Working for Yourself

The Daily Telegraph Guide to Self Employment

Godfrey Golzen

with Helen Steadman, Alexa Stace, Alex Artley,
F O Kemp, M Mendelsohn

Kogan Page

First published 1975,
reprinted twice in 1976
This new, revised edition published 1978
by Kogan Page Limited
120 Pentonville Road, London N1 9JN

Printed and bound in Great Britain by
Redwood Burn Limited
Trowbridge & Esher

ISBN 0 85038 147 9 H/B
ISBN 0 85038 148 7 P/B

Acknowledgements

We should like to thank John Slade and R W Leff for their advice on accountancy and taxation, and all the other freelance and self-employed people who have helped with the compilation of the 'Opportunities' section.

We should be most grateful for readers' comments and suggestions; there are as many different ways of running small businesses as there are proprietors, and any advice on methods other than those we have indicated will be considered for inclusion in future editions of the book.

Safeguard your retirement with a Guarantee Plus Retirement Plan

The Save & Prosper Guarantee Plus Retirement Plan is specifically designed to meet the needs of the self-employed and those who are not covered by an occupational pension scheme.

It provides:–

✳ **A guaranteed pension**

✳ **The prospect of a bonus pension** related to the performance of the investments underlying your plan.

✳ **A tax-free lump sum** You may take part of your pension benefits as a lump sum, which in many cases could exceed your net contributions, and take a reduced pension.

✳ **Tax benefits** In particular, all contributions, within certain limits, are eligible for tax relief at the rates payable on the top slice of your earned income.

Interested? Then ask one of our local branch offices or your professional adviser for further details. Alternatively complete and return the coupon below. We have branches in:–

Birmingham, Brentford, Bristol, Croydon, Edinburgh, Glasgow, Ilford, Leeds, Manchester, Newcastle, Nottingham, Plymouth, Southampton.

Contents

Part 1:
Running Your Own
Business:
A Crash Course

CITY OF WESTMINSTER ASSURANCE

Flexible Pension Plans

Whether you're self-employed or eligible for our Directors and Executives Pension Scheme, City of Westminster Assurance can give you an outstandingly flexible pension plan backed by a highly successful investment record.

When choosing a pension plan, it is vitally important that you should know what your options are. All too many schemes fail to cater adequately for the individual requirements of a particular person.

City of Westminster Assurance, however, has based both its Self-Employed and Director's Pension Plans on the premise that the individual comes first. Freedom of choice is a key factor in both these contracts, allowing investors real flexibility about the way they invest and subsequently draw their benefits.

Ask your broker for details of whichever plan is appropriate for you. And bear in mind that City of Westminster has an excellent long-term investment record backed up by a special reputation for original thinking in the field of pensions and life assurance.

A **SENTRY** INSURANCE GROUP COMPANY

Sentry House, 56 Leadenhall Street, London EC3A 2BJ.

1: Going it Alone

Since the first edition of this book was published in 1975 the climate of political opinion towards the self-employed has changed dramatically for the better. It might be too much to claim that they are the government's darling, but there is a certain amount of consensus by both political parties that the encouragement of small businesses may provide the answer to one of our most worrying problems: chronic unemployment. It has been demonstrated throughout the first half of the seventies that creating jobs in the public sector — the solution favoured by the left — is a vastly expensive one, that, in draining workers from potentially productive areas of the economy, carries the seeds of its own bankruptcy. From an ideological point of view there is also an increasing feeling that a highly bureaucratic corporate state, limiting people's choice about how they spend their money, or even ultimately where and at what they want to work, is a road down which we have travelled far enough. As for the belief that encouraging public and discouraging private ownership would lead to better industrial relations, that pious myth has been destroyed by the countless public sector strikes in the last 30 years.

Yet there is no doubt that unemployment is unacceptably high and that it is here to stay unless we do something about it. In fact it is here to increase, because automation of all kinds of processes, from controlling production lines to checking tins of groceries on supermarket shelves, is not only over the horizon but will soon be within the financial reach of even the smaller firms. More automation means fewer jobs for people and some readers of this book may already have fallen victim to this process. But it also means more uniformity, less flexibility and less choice and this is where the self-employed come into their own as a new kind of labour force, operating at every level from providing specialist consultancy to making goods and selling services that are still needed, but which the big firms with their colossal overheads no longer find it worthwhile to supply. Ironically enough, by the way, among the customers of many small independent companies are some of the big firms themselves — because they find some service or part is unobtainable due to strikes, production hold-ups or because some other big firm has given up producing it. Not infrequently, in fact, they are having to turn to some former employee who has gone into business for himself, having anticipated or had prior knowledge of exactly such a problem.

Often such a man might have been made redundant as a result of technological change — men being replaced by machines. Here the person affected may find two kinds of opportunities for self-employment. The first arises because skills which are obsolete in one context may be greatly in demand in another; a case in point would be middle-level accounting experience, desperately needed by many small firms in the form of a consultancy service. The second because not everyone wants machine-made products off the assembly line. Indeed, all the indications are that as people become more affluent they want more, not less individuality. The insatiable appetite for antiques is not simply due to the fact that they are a good investment. They are also more individual and more human.

It is this human element in self-employment that is increasingly attracting the sort of thinkers who, a decade or so ago, might have been more interested in socialist solutions, and has made even a Labour government look on the self-employed with a kindlier eye. As people become less and less involved in what they produce and are consigned to the role of button-pushers on machines they become alienated from their labour or in simpler terms, fed up — a situation of perpetual boredom which finds expression in strikes, absenteeism, general bloody-mindedness on the factory floor or total lack of interest in the office. There is no way, of course, that we can go back to a society of individual craftsmen without an unacceptable drop in our standards of living. But maybe, so the argument runs, we should leave to machines what machines do best and get human beings to cater to the individual taste, the quirky needs, the one-off problems and the sudden emergencies and breakdowns that machines cannot handle.

This is certainly where the opportunities for the self-

employed lie, and one of the objects of this general pre-
amble is to make an important practical point. The game the
giants play has its limitations, but do not take them on direct.
If for instance, you are a skilled cabinetmaker, don't get into
mass-produced furniture — you simply won't be able to get
your prices down far enough to make a living, nor will you
be able to handle distribution on the scale that mass production implies. Do something the giants don't do, like
making things to individual specifications. If you've always
wanted to own a grocery shop, don't do the same thing as the
supermarket round the corner. Bake your own bread or make
your delicatessen or stay open round the clock — do something you can do better or differently.

How well prepared are you?

Of course, having a sound idea is only part of the story.
How prepared you are to take it further depends on the
extent of your experience; not that it is absolutely essential
at the 'thinking about it' stage to have all-round direct
experience of the sort of self-employment opportunity you
want to exploit. But you have to be aware of what you know
and don't know about it. You may be a manager who is also
a keen gardener and you want to set up a market-gardening
business. In that case you probably have a rather better
knowledge of management essentials than that of a hypothetical competitor who is currently employed by a market
gardener and wants to set up on his own. But on the finer
points of growing techniques and hazards, and where to sell
the products, your competitor is going to be much better
equipped than you.

The first step, therefore, is to make a list of all the aspects
you can think of about running the business — show it to
someone who is already in the field to make sure nothing of
importance has been missed out — tick off the ones you
think you can handle and consider how you are going to deal
with the areas where your experience is limited. The best way
may well be to gain practical first-hand experience. If you are
thinking of buying a shop, for instance, working in one for a
few weeks will teach you an amazing amount about the
public's tastes — what sells and what doesn't — and you may
save yourself hundreds of pounds in making the right buying
decisions later on. As far as management principles are
concerned, your library will provide you with lists for further

reading; and you should also take advice from your local Small Firms Information Centre (see pages 226—227).

The importance of planning

If you are going to borrow money to get your firm off the ground, the lender (if he has any sense!) will want to know how you plan to use his money and if the operation you have in mind is going to give him an adequate return on his investment. This means that you must have a clear idea of how your business is going to develop, at least for the next year, where you see work coming from and whether you are going to have the future resources, human and financial, to handle it.

Even if you don't need to borrow money, planning is vital. Landing a big contract or assignment for a new business is a heartening beginning, but well before work on it is completed you should be looking around for the next job; and the completion dates you have given should take this into account — unless the amount of money you are going to get from it is so much that you will have plenty of time to look around for more work after this first job is done. But that, too, is a matter of planning.

Is self-employment the right career for you?

Let us leave aside Samuel Smiles-like homilies about having to be your own hardest taskmaster. We will take it for granted that you are not considering working for yourself as a soft option. But apart from the question of whether your health can stand the fairly demanding regime that full-time self-employment implies, there are also other questions you have to ask yourself about your aptitude — as opposed to a mere hankering — for going it alone. First of all, there are severely practical considerations: whether you have enough money or the means of raising it. And remember you will need money not only to finance your business or practice, but also for your own personal needs, including sickness and holiday periods.

Self-employment may mean a drop in your standard of living — possibly a permanent one, if things don't go as planned. Are you prepared for that? Is your family going to like it? Have you seriously considered the full price to be paid for independence? Is your wife (or husband) able and willing to lend a hand?

Insecurity, a necessary condition of self-employment, is not everyone's cup of tea. Neither are some of the implications of being your own master. One of the most important of them is the ability to make decisions and if you very much dislike doing this, self-employment is probably not the right channel for your abilities. You are constantly going to be called on to make decisions — some of them rather trivial, where it doesn't matter greatly what you do decide, so long as you decide *something*; but some of them will be fundamental policy decisions that could make or break your business.

You are also going to be called on to make decisions about people, and these are often the hardest of all. It is terribly difficult to sack someone with whom you have worked in the intimacy of a small office, but sooner or later that kind of situation will land in your lap. So another quality that is called for is toughness. This doesn't mean overbearing nastiness, but it does mean the readiness, for instance, to part company with a supplier — even if he is a personal friend — if his product starts to fall consistently below standard.

We have touched on the question of your aptitude for self-employment as such, but there remains the matter of your aptitude for the sphere of activity you have chosen. A management consultant friend of the writer's uses a basic precept in advising companies on personnel problems: staff are best employed doing what they are best at. The same applies to self-employment and most people go into it with that in mind. The problem with self-employment, however, is that at least at the outset you cannot absolutely avoid all the aspects of the work that in a bigger organisation you might have delegated or passed on to another department because you yourself don't much enjoy doing them: keeping books and records is a case in point. What you have to do is to maximise the number of tasks you are good at and minimise the others. This may mean taking a partner to complement your skills or employing an outside agency to handle some things for you: selling, for instance, if you are good at making things but not so good at negotiating or dealing with people. That means less money for you, but at the risk of sounding moralistic, you are unlikely to succeed if making money is the only thing you have in mind and overrides considerations like job satisfaction.

15

At the same time, the costs of doing anything in business must always be taken into account: for example, if you take a partner, is there going to be enough money coming in to make a living for both of you? Unless you constantly quantify your business decisions in this way, you are unlikely to stay in business very long. In fact, you should not even start on your career as a self-employed person without investigating very carefully whether there is a big and lasting enough demand for the product or service you are proposing to offer, and whether it can be sold at a competitive price that will enable you to earn a living after meeting all the expenses of running a business.

In conclusion

If you have faced the issues we have touched on in the last paragraphs and feel confident about dealing with them, then your chances of success in self-employment, whether as a full-timer or as a source of extra income, are good. As for the opportunities, they are legion and in the latter half of the book we have set out what is involved in some of the more popular areas. The list obviously cannot be comprehensive (though it should serve as a stimulus to looking in other directions as well) and neither can the coverage of basic management techniques in the first half. But one of the essentials of effective management is to pick out no more from any topic than you need to know to accomplish the task in hand. We hope that in these chapters we have given you the kind of technical information that you will be concerned with at this early stage of your career as a self-employed person.

Checklist: going it alone

1. Can you measure the demand for your product or service in terms of money?
2. Who are your competitors and what can you offer that they cannot?
3. Is the market local or national and how can you reach it? Can you measure the cost of doing so in financial terms?
4. How much capital have you got and how easy is it to realise?

5. How much money do you need for start-up costs and if it is more than your capital, how can you make up the difference?
6. How long is it likely to be before your income meets your outgoings and how do you propose to manage until then?
7. Do you have any established contacts who can give you business?
8. Is your proposed activity a one-off opportunity or a line for which there is a continuing demand?
9. What aspects of your proposed activity do you have first-hand experience in and how do you propose to fill in the gaps?
10. How good is your health?
11. What are you best at/worst at in your present job and how does this relate to your area of self-employment?
12. Is there any way you can combine your present job with self-employment for an experimental period while you see how it goes?
13. Have you made a realistic appraisal of your aptitude for going it alone, both generally and in the context of the line of work you have chosen?
14. Should you join up with someone else and, if so, is the net income you anticipate going to provide a livelihood for all the people involved?

2: Setting Up Your Business

Before you start talking to bank managers, solicitors, accountants or tax inspectors you will have to start thinking about what sort of legal entity the business you are going to operate is to be. The kind of advice you seek from them will depend on this decision, and you have three choices. You can operate as a sole trader (ie a one-man business — it does not necessarily have to be a 'trade'), a partnership, or as a private limited company. Let us see what each of these options implies.

Sole trader

There is nothing — or at least very little — to stop you from starting a business under your own name, operating from a back room of your own house. But if the place you live in is owned by someone else, you should get the landlord's permission; and if the business you are starting in your home is one that involves a change of use of the premises from domestic to obviously industrial — for instance a manufacturing process involving occasional noise — you will have to get planning permission from the local authority's planning officer. In that case you may also find that you are re-rated on a commercial basis. If you own your house, you should also check that there are no restrictive covenants in the deeds governing its use. On the whole, though, a business conducted unobtrusively from a private residence is unlikely to attract attention from the local authority. To be perfectly safe, however, it may be as well to have a word with the authority's planning department since any change of use, even of part of your residence, requires planning permission.

The next step is to inform your local tax inspector or to

get your accountant to do so. This is always advisable if the nature of your earnings is changing and imperative if you are moving from employee to full-time self-employed status, because it changes the basis on which you pay tax. The inspector will give you some indication of allowable business expenses to be set off against your earnings for tax purposes. These will not include entertainment of potential customers (unless they are overseas buyers) but will cover items 'wholly and exclusively incurred for the purposes of business'. These are spelt out in more detail in Chapter 10. Some things, of course, are used partly for private and partly for business purposes — your car or your telephone, for instance. In these cases only that proportion of expenditure that can definitely be attributed to business use is chargeable against tax. Careful records of such use must, therefore, be kept, and its extent must also be credible. If you are not exporting anything in the way of a product or service, you may be unable to convince the inspector that a weekend in Paris was in the course of business! But if you are, he is unlikely to quibble about a modest hotel bill, even if the business part of your visit only took a couple of hours.

The principal cautionary point to bear in mind about operating as a sole trader is that you are personally liable for the debts of your business. If you go bankrupt your creditors are entitled to seize and sell up your personal possessions, not just equipment, cars and other items directly related to your business.

Partnerships

Most of the above points are also true if you are setting up in partnership with other people. Once again, there are very few restrictions against setting up in partnership with someone to carry on a business, but because all the members of a partnership are personally liable for its debts, even if these are incurred by a piece of mismanagement by one partner which was not known to his colleagues, the choice of partners is a step that requires very careful thought. So should you have a partner at all? Certainly it is not advisable to do so just for the sake of having company, because unless the partner can really contribute something to the business, you are giving away a part of what could in time be a very valuable asset to little purpose. A partner should be able to provide some important angle to running the business which you yourself are unable to take care of. He may have some range of specialised expertise that is vital to the business; or he may have a range of contacts to bring in work; or the work may be of such a nature that the executive tasks and decisions cannot be handled by one person. He may even be a 'sleeping partner' who is doing little else apart from putting up some money in return for a share of the eventual profits.

But whatever the reason for establishing a partnership as opposed to going it alone and owning the whole business may be, you should be sure that your partner (of course, there may be more than one, but for the sake of simplicity we will assume that only one person is involved) is someone you know well in a business, not just a social capacity. Because of this, before formally establishing a partnership, it may be advisable to tackle, as an informal joint venture, one or two jobs with the person you are thinking of setting up with, carrying at the end of the day an agreed share of the costs and profits. That way you will learn about each other's strengths and weaknesses, and indeed whether you can work together harmoniously at all. It may turn out, for instance, that your prospective partner's expertise or contacts, while useful, do not justify giving him a share of the business and that in fact a consultancy fee is the right way of remunerating him.

Even if all goes swimmingly and you find that you can work well together, it is vital that a formal partnership agreement should be drawn up by a solicitor. This is true even of husband-and-wife partnerships. The agreement should cover such points as the following:

1. Who is responsible for what aspects of the operation (eg production, marketing, etc)?
2. What constitutes a policy decision (eg whether or not to take on a contract) and how is it taken? By a majority vote, if there are an uneven number of partners? By the partner concerned with that aspect of things? Only if all partners agree?
3. How are the profits to be divided? According to the amount of capital put in? According to the amount of work done by each partner? Over the whole business done by the partnership over a year? On a job-by-job basis? How much money can be drawn, on what basis, and how often in the way of remuneration?

21

4. What items, like cars, not exclusively used for business can be charged to the partnership? And is there any limitation to the amount of money involved?
5. If one of the partners retires or withdraws how is his share of the business to be valued?
6. If one of the partners dies, what provision should the others make for his widow?

There are obviously many kinds of eventualities that have to be provided for, depending on the kind of business that is going to be carried on. Some professional partnerships, for instance, may consist of little more than an agreement to pool office expenses like the services of typists and telephonists, with each partner drawing his own fees quite independently of the rest. The best way to prepare the ground for a solicitor to draw up an agreement is for each partner to make a list of possible points of dispute and to leave it to the legal adviser to produce a form of words to cover these and any other points he may come up with himself.

Private limited companies

Except when your business or freelance occupation is on a very small scale — something that brings in only a few extra pounds a week — it is generally advisable to set up as a private limited company, unless you are prevented from doing so for professional reasons or if you are under a legal disability such as applies to undischarged bankrupts. The advantage of a limited company is that, in law, it has an identity distinct from that of the shareholders who are its owners. Consequently, if a limited company goes bankrupt, the claims of the creditors are limited to the assets of the company. This includes any capital issued to shareholders which they have either paid for in full or in part. We shall return to the question of share capital in a moment, but the principle at work here is that when shares are issued the shareholders need not necessarily pay for them in full, though they have a legal obligation to do so if the company goes bankrupt. Shareholders are not, however, liable as individuals and their private assets outside the company may not be touched, unless their company has been trading fraudulently.

22

A limited company can be formed by two shareholders (who can be husband and wife), one of whom must be a director. It must also have a company secretary, who can be an outside person, such as your solicitor or accountant. Apart from this, the main requirements relate to documentation. Like sole traders or partnerships, a limited company must prepare a set of accounts annually for the inspector of taxes, but it has the further obligation that these have to be audited, normally by an accountant, who has to certify that they present 'a true and fair view' of the company's finances; and it must make an annual return to the Registrar of Companies, showing all the shareholders and directors, any changes of ownership that have taken place, a profit and loss account over the year and a balance sheet.

The cost of forming a company, including the capital duty which is based on the issued capital (we shall come to the distinction between this and nominal capital shortly) is likely to be around £100, depending on what method you use to go about it. The cheapest way is to buy a 'ready-made' company from one of the registration agents who advertise their services in specialist financial journals. Such a company will not actually have been trading, but will be properly registered by the agents. All that has to be done is for the existing 'shareholders' (who are probably the agent's nominees) to resign and for the purchasers to become the new shareholders and to appoint directors.

Alternatively you can start your own company from scratch, but whichever course you choose professional advice is vital at this stage. The technicalities are trickier than they sound, though simple enough to those versed in such transactions.

Registration of business names

One problem you may encounter with a ready-made company is when it has a name that does not relate meaningfully to the activity you are proposing to carry on. In that case there are two courses open to you:

1. You can apply to the Registrar of Companies (Companies Registration Office, Crown Way, Maindy, Cardiff CF4 3UZ) to change the name. A fee of £10 will be charged for this.
2. You can keep the name of the company, but apply to the Registrar of Business Names to *trade* under a name

23

different from that of the company itself. The addresses of the Registrar of Business Names are:
England and Wales
Pembroke House, 40-56 City Road, London EC1Y 2DN
Scotland
102 George Street, Edinburgh EH2 3DJ
Northern Ireland
43-47 Chichester Street, Belfast BT1 4RJ

The necessity to register the name, either of the company or the business (or both, if they are in any way different) does not only crop up in instances like the one we have just cited, however. If you are intending to set up a company you will have to make application to use the name you have chosen to the Registrar of Companies. Permission will not be granted if it is too much like the name of an existing company, or if the Registrar considers the name is misleading (e g the use of the word 'international' when the firm is plainly not so). The fee for registering a company name is at present £50.

In order to use a *business* name you will have to apply to the Registrar of Business Names and you should do so within 14 days of starting to trade under the name you have chosen. In the case of a limited company application has to be made to use a name other than its existing one or its full corporate one. For instance your company may be called 'John Smith Ltd', but your business name might be 'Regency Antiques'. You will have to apply to use both the *company* name and the *business* name.

In the case of a sole trader or a partnership you will also have to apply to the Registrar of Business Names if the firm is to trade under any other name than that of the people or person concerned, without any qualification or description. (A somewhat sexist touch applies here to married women, who have to apply to the Registrar if they want to trade under their maiden name.) Thus, if you are proposing to trade as plain Tom Jones, it will not be necessary to register the name of your enterprise. But if you are calling your business 'Tom Jones, Design Consultant' you will have to apply to use this name within fourteen days of commencing to trade. The fee at present is £1.

Incidentally, it is worth giving a good deal of thought to the choice of a business name. Clever names are all very well, but if they do not clearly establish the nature of the business you are in, prospective customers leafing through a telephone or business directory may have trouble in finding you; or, if they do find you, they may not readily match your name to their needs. For instance, if you are a furniture repairer, it is far better to describe yourself as such in your business name then to call yourself something like 'Chippendale Restorations'. On the other hand if you already have a big reputation in some specialised sector, stick with it. Arguably, some of the Beatles' business ventures might have been more successful if they had traded on that name, instead of using the label 'Apple' for their other activities.

The rules governing the use of business names are like those for company names, except that the Registrar is less concerned about the fact that a similar trading name may already be in existence. Obviously, however, it is advisable in both cases to wait until the name you have put forward is accepted before having any stationery printed. When you do get to this stage the names of the proprietors (or, in the case of a limited company, the directors) have to be shown not only on letterheads, but also on catalogues and trade literature. Limited companies, in addition, have to show their registration number and the address of their registered office on such stationery.

This address may not necessarily be the same as the one at which business is normally transacted. Some firms use their accountant's or solicitor's premises as their registered office — you will probably see quite a number of registration certificates hanging in their office (they are required by law to be so displayed) when you go there. This is because it is to that address that all legal and official documents are sent. If you have placed complete responsibility for dealing with such matters in the hands of professional advisers it is obviously convenient that the related correspondence should also be directed there. Bear in mind, though, that this does involve a certain loss of control on your part. Unless you at least first see these documents yourself, you will have no idea, for instance, whether the important ones are being handled with due dispatch.

Limited company documents

When you set up a limited company, your solicitor or accountant will be involved in drafting certain papers and documents which govern its structure and the way it is to be run. When this process has been completed you will receive

25

copies of the company's Memorandum and Articles of Association, some share transfer forms, a Minute Book, the Company Seal and the Certificate of Incorporation. Let us explain briefly what these mean.

The Memorandum

This document sets out the main objects for which the company is formed and what it is allowed to do. There are standard clauses for this and your professional adviser will use these in drafting the document. The main thing to watch out for is that he should not be too specific in setting out the limits of the proposed operation, because if you change tack somewhere along the line — for instance if you move from mail order to making goods for the customers you have built up — you may lose the protection of your limited liability unless the Memorandum provides for this. There are, however, catch-all clauses which allow you to trade in pretty much anything or in any manner you like. Furthermore, the 'objects' clauses can be changed by a special resolution, passed by 75 per cent of the shareholders.

The Memorandum also sets out the company's nominal or authorised share capital and the par value per share. This is a point about which many newcomers to this aspect of business get very confused. The thing to remember is that in this context the value of share capital is a purely *nominal* value. You can have a company operating with thousands of pounds' worth of nominal share capital. This sounds very impressive, but what counts is the *issued* share capital, because this represents what the shareholders have actually put into the business or pledged themselves so to do. It is quite possible to have a company with a nominal capital of £1000, but with only two issued shares of £1 each to the two shareholders that are required by law.

The issued share capital also determines the ownership of a company. In the case we have just quoted, the two shareholders would own the company jointly. But if they then issue a third £1 share to another person without issuing any more to themselves they would now only own two-thirds of the company. This is a vital point to remember when raising capital by means of selling shares.

Apart from determining proportions of ownership, issued share capital also signifies how much of their own money the shareholders have put into the company or are prepared to accept liability for. Therefore in raising money from a bank or finance house, the manager there will look closely at the issued share capital. To the extent that he is not satisfied that the liability for the amount he is being asked to put up is adequately backed by issued share capital, he is likely to ask the shareholders to guarantee a loan or overdraft with their own personal assets — for instance by depositing shares they privately hold in a public quoted company or unit trust as security. In the case of a new company without a track record this would, in fact, be the usual procedure.

The nominal share capital of a new small-scale business is usually £100. It can be increased later on, as business grows, on application to the Registrar of Companies. The point of such a move would be to increase the *issued* share capital, for instance, if a new shareholder were to put money into the company. But once again, it should be borne in mind that if the issued share capital was increased to £1000 from £100, and a backer were to buy £900 worth of shares at par value, the original shareholders would only own one-tenth of the business; the fact that they got the whole thing going is quite beside the point.

One last question about issued share capital which sometimes puzzles people. Must you actually hand over money for the shares when you start your own company, as is the case when you buy shares on the stock market, and what happens to it? The answer is: yes — you pay it into the company's bank account because, remember, it has a separate legal identity from the shareholders who own it. However, you need not pay for your shares in full. You can, for instance, pay 50p per share for a hundred £1 shares. The balance of £50 represents your liability if the company goes bankrupt and you only actually have to hand over the money if that happens or if a majority at a shareholders' meeting requires you to do so. The fact that you have not paid in full for shares issued to you does not, however, diminish your entitlement to share in the profits, these being distributed as dividends according to the proportion of share capital issued. The same applies to outside shareholders, so if you are raising money by selling shares to people outside the firm, you should normally ensure that they pay in full for any capital that is issued to them.

The Articles of Association

These are coupled together with the Memorandum, and set out the rules under which the company is run. They govern matters like issue of the share capital, the appointment and powers of directors and the proceedings at general meetings. As in the case of the Memorandum the clauses are largely standard ones, but those relating to the issue of shares should be read carefully. It is most important that there should be a proviso under which any new shares that are issued should be offered first of all to the existing shareholders in the proportion in which they already hold shares. This is particularly so when three or more shareholders are involved, or when you are buying into a company; otherwise the other shareholders can vote to water down your holding in the company whenever they see fit by issuing further shares. For the same reason, there should be a clause under which any shareholder who wants to transfer shares should offer them first of all to the existing shareholders. The Articles of Association also state how the value of the shares is to be determined, the point here being that if the company is successful and makes large profits, the true value of the shares will be much greater than their 'par' value of £1, 50p or whatever. It should be noted, though, that the market valuation of the shares does not increase the liability of shareholders accordingly. In other words, if your £1 'par' shares are actually valued at, say, £50, your liability still remains at £1.

Table A of the Companies Act of 1948, which can be purchased at any HMSO branch, sets out a specimen Memorandum and Articles.

The Minute Book

Company Law requires that a record be kept of the proceedings at both shareholders' and directors' meetings. These proceedings are recorded in the minute book, which is held at the company's registered office. Decisions made at company meetings are signed by the chairman and are legally binding on the directors if they are agreed by a majority. Therefore, any points of procedure that are not covered by the Memorandum and Articles of Association can be written into the minutes and have the force of law, provided that they do not conflict with the former two documents. Thus, the various responsibilities of the directors can be defined and minuted at the first company meeting; so can important matters such as who signs the cheques. It is generally a good idea for these to carry two signatures to be valid.

The Company Seal

The company seal is a metal disc bearing the name of the company in raised letters. The disc is pressed into all official documents and its use on any occasion must be authorised by the directors.

The Certificate of Incorporation

When the wording of the Memorandum and Articles of Association has been agreed and the names of the directors and the size of the nominal capital has been settled your professional adviser will send the documents concerned to the Registrar of Companies. He will issue a Certificate of Incorporation which is, as it were, the birth certificate of your company.

Company directors

When your Certificate of Incorporation arrives you and your fellow shareholders are the owners of a fully fledged private limited company. You will almost certainly also be the directors. This important-sounding title in fact means very little. A director is merely an employee of the company, who is entrusted by the shareholders with the running of it. He need not himself be a shareholder at all; and he can be removed by a vote of the shareholders — which, since each share normally carries one vote, is a good reason for not losing control of your company by issuing a majority shareholding to outsiders.

Another good reason is that since the ownership of the company is in proportion to the issued share capital, so also is the allocation of profits, when you come to make them. If you let control pass to an outsider for the sake of raising a few hundred pounds now — there are other means of raising capital than the sale of shares, as we shall show in Chapter 7 — you will have had all the sweat of getting things

29

going, while only receiving a small part of the rewards. Remember, furthermore, that without control you are only an employee — even if you are called 'managing director'.

Checklist: setting up in business

Sole trader

1. Do you need planning permission to operate from your own home?
2. Does your lease allow you to carry on a trade from the premises you intend to use?
3. If you own the premises, whether or not they are your home as well, are there any restrictive covenants which might prevent you from using them for the purpose intended?
4. Have you notified your tax inspector that the nature of your earnings is changing?
5. Are you aware of the implications of being a sole trader if your business fails?
6. Have you taken steps to register a business name?

Partnerships

1. Points 1-6 above also apply to partnerships. Have you taken care of them?
2. How well do you know your partners — personally and as people to work with?
3. If you do not know them well what evidence do you have about their personal and business qualities?
4. What skills, contacts or other assets (like capital) can they bring into the business?
5. Have you asked your solicitor to draw up a deed of partnership and does it cover all the eventualities you can think of?
6. Have you talked to anybody who is in, or has tried partnership in the same line of business, to see what the snags are?

Private limited companies

1. Do you have the requisite minimum number of shareholders (2)?

as a book-keeper or merely as an 'accountant' is not qualified to give professional advice in the meaning of that term, though a good unqualified man can do a very adequate job in preparing tax returns for something like a small freelance business.

A solicitor will also want to know the kind of business you are in and your plans for the future. But he will concentrate, obviously, on legal rather than financial aspects (so don't go on about money — he is a busy man, and this is only an exploratory visit). He is interested in what structure the operation is going to have and, in the case of a partnership or limited company, whether you and your colleagues have made any tentative agreements between yourselves regarding the running of the firm and the division of profits. He will want to get some idea of what kind of property you want to buy or lease and whether any planning permissions have to be sought.

How much is he going to charge?

A question like that is rather like asking how long a piece of string is. It depends on how often you have to consult your adviser, so it is no use asking him to quote a price at the outset, though if you are lucky enough to have a very clear idea of what you want done — say, in the case of an accountant, a monthly or weekly supervision of your books, plus the preparation and auditing of your accounts — he may give you a rough idea of what his charges will be. Alternatively he may suggest an annual retainer for these services and any advice directly concerned with them, plus extra charges for anything that falls outside them, like a complicated wrangle with the inspector of taxes about allowable items.

An annual retainer is a less suitable way of dealing with your solicitor because your problems are likely to be less predictable than those connected with accounting and book-keeping. A lot of your queries may be raised, and settled, on the telephone: the 'Can I do this?' type. Explaining that kind of problem on the telephone is usually quicker and points can be more readily clarified than by writing a letter setting out the facts of the case (though you should ask for confirmation in writing in matters where you could be legally liable in acting on the advice you have been given!). However, asking advice on the telephone can be embarrassing for both parties. You will be wondering whether your solicitor is charging you for it and either way it could inhibit you from thrashing the matter out fully. Therefore you should check at the outset what the procedure is for telephone enquiries and how these are accounted for on your bill.

A guide — not a crutch

For someone starting in business on their own, facing for the first time 'the loneliness of thought and the agony of decision', there is a temptation to lean on professional advisers too much. Apart from the fact that this can be very expensive, it is a bad way to run a business. Before you lift the telephone or write a letter, think. Is this clause in a contract something you could figure out for yourself if you sat down and concentrated on reading it carefully? Wouldn't it be better to check through the ledger yourself to find out where to put some item of expenditure that is not immediately classifiable? Only get in touch with your advisers when you are genuinely stumped for an answer — not just because you can't be bothered to think it out for yourself. Remember, too, that nobody can make up your mind for you on matters of policy. If you feel, for instance, that you can't work with your partner, the only thing your solicitor can or should do for you is to tell you how to dissolve the partnership — not whether it should be done at all.

Your bank manager

The other person with whom you should make contact when you start up in business is your bank manager. The importance of picking a unit of the right size which we have mentioned in connection with professional advice also holds true in this case. A smaller local branch is more likely to be helpful towards the problems of a small business than one in a central urban location with a lot of big accounts among its customers. You might also discuss, with your accountant, the possibility of going outside the 'big five'. It is necessary to be careful here because there have been some recent failures of 'fringe banks', but there are a number of solid smaller banking houses who are more accommodating about charges on handling your account and loans. Of course, if you are changing banks — as opposed to merely switching branches — it will be difficult for you to get a sizeable overdraft until the manager has seen something of your track record.

The question of obtaining bank loans or overdrafts is dealt with more fully in Chapter 7, but in the first instance you should inform your bank manager of your intentions to set up in business, providing him with much the same information as you provided to your accountant. Indeed it is quite a good idea to ask your accountant to come along to this first meeting, so that he can explain any technicalities.

Of course, you may be operating a small-scale freelance business that does not call for bank finance. It is still a good idea, in that case, to keep your personal and business accounts separate, with separate cheque and paying-in books for each one. Mixing up private and business transactions can only lead to confusion, for yourself as well as your accountant.

Insurance

If you are setting up a photographic studio and an electrical fault on the first day destroys some of your equipment you are in trouble before you have got going. If you are a decorator and a pot of paint falling from a window sill causes injury to someone passing below you could face a suit for damages that will clean you out of the funds you have accumulated to start your business. Therefore insurance coverage is essential from the start for almost all kinds of business.

Insurance companies vary a good deal in the premiums they charge for different kinds of cover; also in the promptness with which they pay out on claims. Therefore the best plan is not to go direct to a company — even if you already transact your car or life insurance with them — but to an insurance broker. Brokers receive their income from commissions from the insurance companies they represent, but they are generally independent of individual companies and thus reasonably impartial. Here again, your accountant or solicitor can advise you of a suitable choice, which would be a firm that is big enough to have contacts in all the fields for which you need cover (and big enough to exert pressure on your behalf when it comes to making a claim) but not so big that the relatively modest amounts of commission they will earn from you initially are not worth their while taking too much trouble over — for instance when it comes to reminding you about renewals. Apart from these general points, you will have to consider what kinds of cover you need and this will vary somewhat with the kind of business you are in. The main kinds are:

1. Insurance of your premises.
2. Insurance of the contents of your premises.
3. Insurance of your stock.
   (The above three kinds of cover should also extend to 'consequential loss'. For instance, you may lose in a fire a list of all your customers. This list has no value in itself but the 'consequent' loss of business could be disastrous. The same is true of stock losses. If a publisher loses all his books in a fire it is not only their value that affects him, but the consequent loss of business while they are being reprinted — by which time the demand for them may have diminished.)
4. Employer's liability if you employ staff on the premises, even on a part-time basis.
5. Public liability in case you cause injury to a member of the public or his premises in the course of business. You will also need third-party public liability if you employ staff or work with partners.

Your broker will advise you on other items of cover you will need — some professions, for instance, need professional liability cover — but do not leave the whole business of insurance in his hands. Read your policies carefully when you get them and make sure that the fine print does not exclude any essential item.

Insurance is expensive — though the premiums are, of course, allowable against tax inasmuch as they are incurred wholly in respect of your business — and you may find that in the course of time you have paid out thousands of pounds without ever making a claim. However, it is a vital precaution, because one fire or legal action against you can wipe out the work of years if you are not insured. For this reason you must check each year that items like contents insurance represent current replacement values and that your premiums are paid on the due date. Your broker should remind you about this, but if he overlooks it, it is you who carries the can.

Checklist: professional advisers

Solicitors

1. How well do you know the firm concerned?
2. What do you know of their ability to handle the kind of transactions you have in mind?
3. Is their office convenient to the place of work you intend to establish?
4. Do they know local conditions and personalities?
5. Are they the right size to handle your business affairs over the foreseeable future?
6. Have you prepared an exhaustive list of the points on which you want legal advice at the setting-up stage?

Accountants

1. Have they been recommended by someone whose judgement you trust and who has actually used their services?
2. Are the partners members of one of the official accountants' bodies? If not, are you satisfied that they can handle business on the scale envisaged?
3. Is their office reasonably close by?
4. Does it create a good and organised impression?
5. Can they guarantee that a member of the firm will give you personal and reasonably prompt attention when required?
6. Have you thought out what sort of help you are going to need?
7. Have you prepared an outline of your present financial position and future needs?
8. Have you considered in consultation with your solicitor, whether you want to set up as a sole trader, a partnership or a limited company?

Bank manager

1. Is your present bank likely to be the right one for you to deal with in this context?
2. Have you informed your bank manager of your intention to set up a business?
3. Have you established a separate bank account for your business?
4. Have you discussed with your bank manager the possibility of switching your account to a local, smaller branch?

Insurance

1. Do you have a reliable reference on the broker you intend to use?
2. Is he efficient, according to the reports you receive, about reminding you when policies come up for renewal?
3. Has he any track record of paying promptly on claims?
4. Have you prepared a list of the aspects of your proposed business which require insurance cover?
5. Are you fully insured for replacement value and consequential loss?
6. Have you read the fine print on your policies or checked them out with your solicitors?

4: Simple Accounting Systems and their Uses

Any bank manager will tell you that at least 80 per cent of all business failures are caused by inadequate record-keeping. Unfortunately this fault is by no means uncommon in small businesses because the entrepreneurial person who tends to set up on his own is often temperamentally different from the patient administrative type who enjoys paperwork and charting information in the form of business records. He is apt to feel what really keeps the show on the road is obtaining and doing the work, or being in the shop to look after customers. However, unless you document money coming in and going out, owed and owing, you will never have more than the haziest idea of how much to charge for your products or services, where your most profitable areas of activity are (and indeed whether you are making a profit at all), how much you can afford to pay yourself and whether there is enough cash coming in to cover immediate commitments in the way of wages, trade debts, tax or professional fees, rent, rates, etc.

Legally, in fact, only a limited company is obliged to keep proper books of account: the definition is that they have to do so 'with respect to all receipts and expenses, sales and purchases, assets and liabilities and they must be sufficient to give a true and fair picture of the state of the company's affairs and to explain its transactions'. But this is no bad objective for anyone carrying on business on a full-time basis; and even part-timers should keep some basic records because they provide essential documentation for your tax return and in the case of VAT (see pages 114-116) the claim for re-payment of any VAT you have paid for goods or services received.

Two starting points

A useful base to start from, particularly for the one-man, service-oriented operation like a design consultant, is an ordinary notebook which is always carried around with you. It is only too easy to forget things by the end of the day — materials bought, fares and petrol, jobs undertaken and their deadlines, cash payments from customers. Details of jobs should be transferred to your desk diary. Cash items — payments and receipts — should be transferred to the cash book to which we shall come in a moment. You should also note the kind of small payments for which no receipt is issued — bus fares, for instance. Incurred in the course of business, they are tax deductible and can add up to a lot of money in the course of the year.

For larger outlays you may find credit cards a useful record-keeping aid. Apart from the fact that when card companies render their account for payment they provide a breakdown of where, when, and how what items were purchased they also, in effect, give you six weeks' credit. With inflation running at around 1½ per cent a month, as it has done in the recent past, this is a real consideration.

The other useful basic item for a small business is a 'spike' on which incoming receipts, invoices, statements and delivery notes can be placed. This ensures that such documents are kept together — not used to put cups on, or carried around in your wallet for making odd notes on the back! The spike should be supplemented by a spring-loaded box file, and at the end of the day all these documents should be placed in the file, with each day separated by a dated sheet of paper.

Ready-made account books

The best method of keeping your books will vary widely between the kind of business you are in and the scale of it. For instance a shop doing most of its business in cash across the counter will need different records from those of a manufacturer or a mail-order firm; an interior designer who supplies the materials with which his designs are executed will need to record more information than one who acts purely as a consultant. Your accountant will advise you on these points, but he may well suggest, if you are running a small operation, that you invest in one of the ready-made account books that can be bought at W H Smith or any other large stationer. Two of the most widely-used ones are the *Complete Traders Account Book* and the *Self-employed Account Book*, both produced by Collins at around £3.50 (at the time of writing). The former is more suitable for retailers. Both contain a page for every week of the year, with ample space for recording receipts and payments, for analysing payments by cheque and for recording VAT inputs. They are clearly set out, easy to follow and worked examples are given.

A system of your own

If you find that neither of these books (and there are others) quite fits the bill you can devise a system of your own. How complex it has to be depends on the nature and size of your business, so you should ask your accountant what books he advises you to keep. However, a very simple system for a small business could be built around five basic types of record.

Cash book Shows all payments received and made, with separate columns for cash transactions and those made through the bank (ie payments by cheque). Amounts received from customers are credited to their account in the ledger (see below). Payments made to suppliers are debited to their account in the ledger.

Petty cash book Shows expenditure on minor items – postage, fares, entertainment and so forth, with a column for VAT.

Sales day book Records invoices sent out to customers in date order, with some analysis of the goods or service supplied and a column for VAT.

Purchases day book Records similar information about purchases.

Ledger Sets out details, taken from sales and purchases day books, of individual customers' and suppliers' accounts and serves as a record of amounts owed and owing. Details from the analysis columns of the sales and purchases day books are also transcribed, usually monthly, under corresponding headings in the ledger. This enables you to see at a glance where your sales are coming from and where your money is going.

Let us look at each of these books a little more closely to see in broad outline what is involved in entering them up and how they link together to enable you to keep track of payments and receipts.

The cash book

Like the ready-made books of account, you can buy this at any business stationer's. The kind of simple book you should select will be divided vertically into two sections. On the left-hand side you enter payments received. There are columns for the date, who the payment was from and how much it was. This last item is divided into two headings: Cash and Bank. If payment was received in cash, it goes into the Cash column. If it was in the form of a cheque it goes into the Bank column, assuming you pay your cheques into the bank daily rather than holding them, since this ensures rapid transfer from your customer's account to yours. There is also a further column in which you should put the number of the relevant folio in the ledger when you credit that payment to the customer's account.

In the right-hand section of the cash book you enter payments you make — again showing date, who the payment was made to, the folio number in the ledger of the supplier's account to be debited and whether it was a cash or a bank transaction. In the right-hand section it is also a good idea to have a column recording cheque numbers, since bank statements nowadays merely show those numbers and do not give particulars of whom the cheque was paid to.

Obviously, there will be frequent occasions when you pay cash into the bank or take cash out. Although it is your own money you are moving around, you still have to record these transactions in the cash book. The procedure is that when you take money out of the bank in order to, for instance, top up the petty cash box, you put 'cash from bank' in the column on the left-hand side recording where payments received came from and you enter the amount in the *cash* column, because it is a payment received from the point of view of your cash position. In the right-hand section, which records payments made, you put 'to cash' and enter the amount in the *bank* column — because payment is being made *to* cash *from* bank.

When you put cash into the bank — say after cashing up

Date	Received from	Folio No.	Cash	Bank	Date	Paid to	Folio No.	Cash	Bank
			£	£				£	£
24.2	Opening balance	—	23	987	24.2	Antique Restorers Ltd			83
	A. Brown			27		High Street Auctions			117
	Cash sales		18						
25.2	I. Smith Fine Art Gallery			40	25.2	Cash payment Blackwell's Bookshop		25	10
	Cash sales		53	100					
26.2	D. Jones			34	26.2	Newtown Gazette			30
	Cash sales		43			High St. Motors			18
	Haywards Ltd			18		To bank		100	
	Cash to bank			100					
27.2	Nightingale Ltd			13	27.2	Office Suppliers Ltd			8
	Cash sales		17			Cash payment		33	
28.2	Cash from bank		120		28.2	To cash			120
	Old Time Antiques Ltd			53		Rent			80
						Wages		100	
			274	1372				258	466

Figure 1. *A typical week's entries in the cash book of an antique shop.*

the till — the procedure is reversed. You put 'to bank' in the right-hand section showing payments made and enter the amount in the cash column. In the left-hand side you enter the amount in the bank column and put 'cash to bank'.

A week's entries in the cash book of an antique shop might look like the example in Figure 1. Note that by totalling up the cash and bank columns on each side of the cash book and deducting the right-hand side, showing payments made, from the left-hand side, showing payments received, a total of cash in hand and at the bank can be derived. This would then be the opening balance for next week's entry.

The petty cash book

Petty cash is often regarded as a bit of a joke, but you would be ill-advised to dip into the petty cash box without leaving a slip of paper showing for what purpose the money was taken, the date and the amount. Unless you are able to show that it was used for business purposes the tax inspector will probably take the view that it has gone on private expenditure and you will not be able to set it against tax or to get back any VAT incurred. There is, of course, no harm in taking money out of petty cash to get a packet of cigarettes around the corner, so long as the slip of paper you then deposit states that the amount is to be entered in the 'drawings account' in the ledger which records items personal to the proprietor.

The petty cash book is most conveniently entered up at the end of the week. The 'payments in' column in the left-hand side usually only shows the sum taken from the bank to top up the petty cash and this is also recorded in the cash book as shown in the previous section.

On the right-hand side payments made are recorded — the date, the details, the amount including VAT, and the VAT element by itself. Further columns would provide an analysis of what the money was spent on — travel, entertainment, stamps or whatever — and the totals at the end of the week would be transferred to the relevant account in the ledger. Therefore, against each total, the folio number in the ledger where this amount has been entered is noted.

A week's entry in the petty cash book of the business above might look like the example in Figure 2.

Date	Amount Paid In	Date	Details	Total inc. VAT	VAT	Travel	Entertainment	Postage	Sundries
24.2	£40	24.2	Petrol	£4.00	£1.00	£3.00			
		25.2	Entertainment	£5.36	.42		£4.94		
		26.2	Taxis	£2.16	.17	£1.99			
		27.2	Stamps	£2.00	—			£2.00	
		28.2	Price Stickers	£1.00	.08				.92
			Balance	£14.52					
	£40			£25.48	£1.67	£4.99	£4.94	£2.00	.92
					L2	L17	L18	L19	L7
3.3	Bal b/d £25.48								

Figure 2. *A typical entry in a petty cash book.*

48

Date	Details	Ledger Ref.	Total inc. VAT £	VAT £	Furniture £	Pottery £	Pictures £
24.2	A. Bee Windsor Chair	L33	32.40	2.40	30		
25.2	V. Camp Derby figure	L16	46.44	3.44		43.00	
	Hackenschmidt Galleries, New York 18thC Portrait	L27	200	—			200
			278.84	5.84	30	43.00	200.00

Figure 3. *An example of sales day book entries.*

Note: (1) The last item carries no VAT since it is an export — see Chapter 10; (2) though the sum debited to the customer's ledger will be the amount including VAT, the analysis of sales by category excludes VAT, because the VAT will have to be remitted to Customs and Excise. The VAT account is a separate entry in the ledger.

49

The sales day book

The sales day book provides a record of invoiced sales in date order — that is, sales which are not cash-across-the-counter transactions. You will, of course, have to be able to issue invoices if your business involves giving credit in this way, but if you are operating on a small scale there is no need to get them printed. You can buy perfectly adequate sets of duplicate invoices at W H Smith. In issuing them, be sure to remember to put down your VAT number as well.

The sales day book has vertical columns for the date, the name of the customer and what goods he bought, a ledger reference number (the amount on the invoice is subsequently debited to the customer's account in the ledger), the amount, the VAT and a number of analysis columns. A typical set of entries in a sales day book might look as in Figure 3.

The purchases day book

The purchases day book is a record of invoices received — that is what you have bought, other than goods supplied for cash. It is set out in much the same way as the sales day book, with the analysis columns itemising the various headings under which the expenditure has been incurred. The amounts for which you have been invoiced are credited to the supplier's account in the ledger.

In all probability you will also give or receive credit for goods that are faulty or wrongly supplied. These are entered in red in the appropriate columns.

The ledger

Up to this point the details of what you owe your suppliers and what your customers owe you is somewhat scattered and one of the ledger's prime functions is to draw it together. Ideally each customer or supplier should have a ledger page to himself, and since their ranks are liable to be subject to changes and additions, it is usually a good idea to have the ledger in loose-leaf form.

As far as customers are concerned, the amounts invoiced are *debited* — transcribed to the left-hand side of the customer's account with reference number of the transaction in the sales day book. Then, when he pays, that amount is *credited* — transcribed to the right-hand side with the

E. Brown, 36 Copeland Road, Ennywear, Staffs.						
			£			£
Jan 10	Book case	SDB1	54	Jan 11	Cheque	CB2	90
Jan 23	Pair silver candlesticks	SDB3	70	Jan 20	Cheque	CB3	20
			———	Balance c/d			14
			124				———
Feb 1	Balance b/d		14				124

Figure 4. *Typical ledger entries.*

relevant folio number from the cash book. At the end of the month, the figures on each side are totalled up and the balance left unpaid is debited to the opening of the next month. It would look something like Figure 4.

The balance on each account represents the amount owing by a customer or due to a supplier.

Apart from supplier's and customer's accounts you can have pages in your ledgers devoted to various items of expenditure incurred in running your business and drawn from the analysis columns in your petty cash book and sales and purchases day books. The totals of these analysis columns are transcribed (usually monthly) to the accounts for VAT, Rent, Travel, Repairs and whatever other items you want to keep track of in this way.

Capital goods

If you own expensive capital equipment — cars, lorries, machine tools, high-class film or photographic cameras are typical examples — you should have separate accounts for them in the ledger because the method of accounting for them is somewhat different. Capital items depreciate over a period of time (as you will know if you have ever sold a car) and this fact must be reflected both in your balance sheet and in the way you price your goods and services — a point we shall return to in Chapter 8.

Date	Supplier Details	Amount	Date	
1.1.77	Carburettor Delivery Motors van Purchase Price £3000 Depreciation £750 Book value at 31.12.77	£3000 £2250	31.12.78	Deprecia- tion (25%) £750

Figure 5. *Ledger entries for capital goods.*

On the left-hand side you show the date and purchase price. On the right-hand side — this is a once-yearly exercise — the percentage of depreciation and the amount. There are various methods of depreciating capital equipment and your accountant will advise you what formula to adopt.

Trading account

From the books described above you can draw together the information needed to compile the trading account and profit and loss account. The function of the trading account is to tell you whether you have been making a gross profit on your trading. It must be compiled annually and preferably more often than that — quarterly for instance — to enable you to measure your progress.

To put together a trading account you begin by identifying the period you want to cover. Then total up the value of all the sales, whether paid for or not, from the sales account in the ledger and add to them the value of your stock (based on cost or market value, whichever is the lower) at the end of the period. These go on the right-hand side of the trading account. On the left-hand side you put down your opening stock at the beginning of the period and add to it the purchases made since then (from the purchases account in the ledger). Deducting opening stock plus purchases from sales plus closing stock will give you your gross trading profit (or loss) over the period.

Profit and loss account

From this information you can compile the profit and loss account over the same period. The gross profit figure from your trading account goes into the right-hand column and you set against it all the items from the various expenditure accounts in the ledger. You also include in this figure the depreciation on capital equipment — but not its actual cost (even if you purchased it during the period in question) because that crops up later, in the balance sheet.

Deducting the left-hand total from the right-hand total gives you your profit over the period. If the total expenditure exceeds the gross profit you have obviously incurred a loss.

The balance sheet

We have mentioned in the previous section that capital equipment does not figure in the profit and loss account, but goes into the balance sheet. The balance sheet is a picture, taken at a particular point in the year (usually the end of a company's financial year) of what the firm *owes* and what it *owns*. (This is not the same as a profit and loss account, which covers a period of time.) Indeed it is quite possible for a firm to have been making a loss on its profit and loss

Trading Account for Year Ended 31.12.77

	£		£
Opening stock at 1.1.74	2,000	Sales	20,000
Net purchases (less		Closing stock at	
credits, etc.)	12,000	31.12.74	3,000
Gross profit	9,000		
	23,000		23,000

Profit and Loss Account for Year Ended 31.12.77

Rent and rates	1,000	Gross profit	9,000
Salaries	2,750		
Heat, light	200		
Phone	120		
Travel	300		
Repairs	200		
Depreciation	650		
Professional advice	150		
	5,370		
Net profit	3,630		
	9,000		9,000

Figure 6. *Examples of trading account and profit and loss account.*

account, but for what it owns (its assets) to exceed what it owes (its liabilities).

In a balance sheet the assets of the firm usually go on the right and the liabilities on the left. However, all the assets and all the liabilities are generally not lumped together, but distinguished qualitatively by the words 'fixed' and 'current'.

'Fixed assets' are items which are permanently necessary for the business to function — eg machinery, cars, fixtures and fittings, your premises or the lease on them. 'Current assets' on the other hand are things from which cash will be realised in the course of your trading activities. These include amounts owed to you by your debtors (from the customers' accounts in the ledger), and the value of your stock (from the trading account). It also, of course, includes cash at the bank (from the cash book).

With liabilities, the position is reversed. 'Fixed liabilities' are those which you do not have to repay immediately, like a

Balance Sheet as at 31.12.77

Liabilities			Assets		
Capital			*Fixed assets*		
500 Shares of £1 each	£500		Vehicle less	£1600	
Profit	£3630		depreciation	£400	£1200
		£4130	Fixtures and fittings less	£1000	
Fixed liabilities			depreciation	£250	£750
Loan repayable 1980	£1000				£1950
Current liabilities			*Current assets*		
Trade creditors	£795		Stock	£3000	
		£1795	Debtors	£900	
			Cash	£75	£3975
		£5925			£5925

Figure 7. *An example of a balance sheet.*

long-term loan from a kindly relative. What you do have to repay promptly, however, is the interest on that loan and this goes under current liabilities if it is due, but has not been paid at the time the balance sheet has been prepared. The same is true of any amounts you owe to your suppliers' accounts in the ledger. Another item that goes on the 'liabilities' side is the share capital in the business and the profit from the trading account because both these amounts are ultimately owed by the company to the shareholders. Where, on the other hand, the company has been making a loss, the amount is deducted either from profits retained from earlier periods or from the shareholder's capital.

So what should you be looking for in your records?

Obviously you will want to know whether you are making or losing money, but there are many other useful bits of information to be gleaned as well.

OK, so you're making a profit. But what relationship does it bear to the capital employed in the business — which you can calculate by subtracting total liabilities from total assets? Because if you are making less than a 15 per cent return on capital, what with inflation currently running at over that percentage, you aren't, on the face of things, making much progress — though of course, you could be paying yourself a very handsome salary before the profit figure was arrived at.

The percentage return on capital can be calculated by the following sum:

$$\frac{profit}{capital\ employed} \times 100$$

Another thing you can work out from your balance sheet is whether you are maintaining sufficient working capital to meet your requirements for new stock or materials or to pay for wages and rent. Here you look at current assets and current liabilities. The sum:

$$\frac{current\ assets}{current\ liabilities}$$

gives you your *current* ratio. If you have, say, £1000 of each you are said to have a current ratio of 1:1. Clearly in that case you would be in trouble if a major debtor were to go bankrupt. So it may be that you should cut back on some item of expenditure you were planning on.

Furthermore the current ratio includes certain items, like stocks, which may not be immediately realisable. If your current ratio is low, and you are still in two minds whether or not to buy that new machine you might apply what is known as the *acid test ratio*, which shows your ability to meet liabilities quickly if the need arises. Here you simply deduct stock from your figure for current assets to give you a figure for liquid assets ie debtors and cash. If the ratio liquid assets : current liabilities is too low you may have more money tied up in stock than you should have.

Of course, even the acid test ratio assumes that your

debtors are going to pay you in a reasonable period of time: most likely within the terms of trade you are allowing. But is this assumption really correct? Look at the annual sum

$$\frac{\text{debtors}}{\text{sales}} \times 365.$$

If your sales are £10,000 and your debtors owe £1000, then they are near enough meeting net monthly terms for you not to worry about it. But if your debtors, on the same sales turnover, are running to, say £3000, there is something very far wrong with your credit control and you are probably heading for serious trouble.

Another important ratio is profit : sales. What this should be depends on the sort of business you are in. Your accountant should be able to advise you here on the basis of his knowledge of similar traders. If your percentage is on the low side you may be buying badly, failing to pass on cost increases, or possibly incurring losses from pilferage.

There are a lot of other ratios you can look out for, but we hope that you will now be clear that the balance sheet and trading and profit and loss accounts are not just a financial rigmarole you have to go through, but very valuable indicators of the way your business is going — or some other business you are thinking of buying.

They are also useful for:

1. Assisting the bank manager to determine the terms of an overdraft.
2. Selling your business to a proposed purchaser.
3. Agreeing tax liabilities with the inspector of taxes.

Checklist: simple accounting systems

1. Do you carry a notebook to record smaller items of business expenditure (eg taxis) as soon as they are incurred?
2. Have you considered using credit cards for larger outlays?
3. Do you have a system for filing incoming invoices as soon as they are received?
4. Have you asked your accountant what books and records he advises you to keep?
5. Do you know and understand the procedures involved?

If not, have you asked your accountant to recommend someone who can help you on a regular basis — at least once a week or once a month, depending on your scale of operations?

6. Do you have any idea of the ratios current in your type of business, so that you can measure your performance against the norm?

How to Pay Yourself instead of the Tax Man

If you are self-employed or if you earn fees or, in fact, if you are one of the many thousands who will be relying on only a state pension scheme, you may well be entitled to take advantage of one particularly favourable tax concession.

The Government encourages you to provide for your retirement by allowing you tax relief on pension contributions *at the highest rates of tax you pay on your earnings.* The Hill Samuel Life Personal Retirement Plan has been designed to take full advantage of this concession.

Not only that but the contributions are invested in Hill Samuel Pension Funds which are accumulating free of capital gains tax and taxes on income to build up retirement benefits – a tax free lump sum *and* a pension.

In addition to all the tax-saving benefits of an approved self-employed retirement scheme, the Hill Samuel Personal Retirement Plan adds something extra. Choice.

Depending on your own wishes and circumstances, you may choose between a plan with a built-in guarantee and plans which, although involving investment fluctuations, may be considered more likely to cope with inflation over the long term.

Each offers the full tax benefits. And *each* offers the special advantage of Hill Samuel Life's skill and long experience in investment and annuities.

Please send the coupon for details.

5: Invoicing and Credit Control

Time is money, as an old saying goes; and it ought to be written large in the minds of anyone giving credit — any business, that is, that supplies goods and services which are not on a strictly cash-on-the-nail basis.

In these days of tight money there is a tendency for many customers, including large and reputable firms, to delay payment as long as possible; because, as we shall show in Chapter 7, taking credit long — and preferably giving it short — is one way to maintain a flow of cash in the business. The supplier who does not demonstrate that he is in a hurry for payment, therefore, is the one who comes last in the queue.

Sending out invoices and statements

The first step towards ensuring that you are not in this position is to issue an invoice for work done or goods supplied as soon as possible after you deliver. On the invoice you should state your terms — that is, when you expect to receive payment. The usual period is between seven and 30 days after delivery. Many private individuals, in fact, pay on receipt of an invoice. Business firms, on the other hand, expect to receive a statement of their account at the end of the month, setting out invoices due or sent during this period: their dates, invoice number, the nature of the goods and the amount. You can have statement forms printed, but if you are not a limited company you can use your letterheads for this purpose, simply typing the word STATE-MENT at the top. Every customer who has received an invoice and not paid at the end of the month when it is due should get a statement.

The particulars of the invoice(s) are drawn from your customers' ledger, though it is essential to keep copies of the actual invoices as well, filed in date order. You are going to need them for VAT purposes, or to check queries. When you receive payment, check that it tallies with the amount due on the customer's ledger entry, mark off the details against each individual item as shown in the previous chapter and enter the amount in the cash book. If the customer requires a receipt, ask him to return the statement (or the invoice if he has paid on that) with his remittance — otherwise you will be involved in time-consuming typing — tick off the items paid, and attach a receipt form or bang on a rubber stamp, 'Paid'. By the way, be uniform about your systems. If you have two different ones for the same part of your operation you are going to waste a lot of time looking in the wrong place when you come to check a document.

Do not neglect the process of checking payments because any amounts unpaid must go into next month's statement. Some invoices which have appeared on your statement will not be paid because they are not yet due for payment. For instance, if your terms are 30 days and you have invoiced an item on the 20th of the month, a business customer is unlikely to pay you until the month following: quite often he only activates payments at the end of the month, unless he is unusually punctilious, efficient or being offered extra discount for quick settlement.

What happens if payment becomes overdue? This is extremely annoying, because at best it is going to involve you in extra correspondence. There are usually three stages. The first is a polite reminder of the amount due, how long it has been due and of your terms of supply. This should be coupled with asking the customer whether he has any queries on any of the invoices which might explain the delay. If there is not a reply by the end of that month, write again, referring to your first reminder and setting a deadline for payment. A telephone call to the customer is often opportune at this stage. If that deadline is not met, you will have to write again, referring to your previous reminders and threatening legal action unless a new and final deadline is met. (If you have a large number of credit accounts, it may pay you to have sets of blank letters for each stage prepared in advance.)

In most cases the threat of legal action will do the trick, but whether you actually carry out your threat will depend on the amount involved. Sums under £50 are not really worth pursuing because your solicitor's services are going to cost you money; and it is not worth taking matters to court — that is, to the stage beyond a solicitor's letter — unless quite a sizeable sum is involved. Your solicitor will advise you on your best course of action. Alternatively, there are firms of debt collectors who are geared to this kind of work and who will endeavour to collect debts for a percentage of the amount due. Five per cent is the norm. But there are some 'cowboys' and a good deal of tricky legislation in debt collecting and you would be well advised to check out any agency that has not been personally recommended with the National Association of Trade Protection Societies, 8 New Street, Leicester LE1 5NF.

You can, of course, ask for references before giving credit though this is a matter which has to be approached with some delicacy; but if you receive a sizeable order out of the blue from some business firm with whom you have not previously dealt, it is advisable to ask for a couple of references in acknowledging the order. Ask the referees to what amount they give credit to this particular customer, how long they have been doing business with him and whether he pays promptly.

If your business consists of making or repairing goods to order — tailoring, for instance — it is not unusual to ask the customer to pay up to 50 per cent on account where an estimate of over £25 or so has been given. This helps cash flow as well as protecting you against possible default. Equally, if goods of resaleable value are left with you for repair you should display a notice reserving the right to dispose of them if the customer does not come to collect them within a reasonable time of completion of the work.

Incidentally a common delaying tactic — or it may be a perfectly legitimate query — is for the customer to ask for copy invoices on receipt of your statement. Do not part with your file copy. You will have to send a photocopy if you do not keep duplicates for this purpose.

Credit cards

For larger personal transactions and for items like the

settlement of restaurant bills credit cards are becoming an increasingly popular method of making payment. A typical scheme is the one operated by the Joint Credit Card Companies, which include ACCESS. The way it works is that a business which wants to offer credit card payment facilities to its customers has to make application to join the scheme to the Joint Credit Card Companies, General Sales Office, 30—31 Newman Street, London W1P 4LJ. The Joint Credit Card Companies then set a money limit to the transaction per customer for which the business in question can accept payment on the cards of JCC member companies. Above that limit, which is based roughly on the applicant's average transaction per customer, the sale has to be referred back to JCC. This can be done over the telephone.

Each sale, as it is made, is entered up on a voucher supplied by the credit card company. The voucher is paid into the bank by the seller and the amount is debited to the card holder's bank account. The advantage of credit cards from the seller's point of view is that he gets guaranteed payment. Against this, he has to pay a small percentage on every transaction to the bank, the amount of this percentage being negotiated at the time he joins the scheme.

Most credit card companies operate on lines very similar to the scheme we have just outlined. Diner's Club vouchers, for instance, though not paid into a bank are sent to the Club organisation on certain specified dates, whereupon payment is made to the seller.

Checking incoming invoices and statements

Unless you transact all your business by paying in cash or by cheque on the spot — and you would be ill-advised to do this — you will also be at the receiving end of invoices and statements from your suppliers. The moment they come in, put them on the spike. Then, daily if possible, enter the details in the supplier's ledger, as described in Chapter 4. File incoming invoices in date order — you will need them for VAT purposes.

When you receive your statement make sure it tallies with the amounts and details which you have entered in the suppliers' ledger, mark off all the items paid and write up the amount in the cash book.

If you are paying by cheque there is no need to ask for a

receipt — it only adds to the paperwork — since an honoured cheque is itself a receipt. Make sure, though, that you enter up the stubs, unless you write up the cash book at the same time as you draw the cheques.

Checklist: invoicing and credit control

Invoicing

1. Are you invoicing promptly, on or with delivery?
2. Do your invoices clearly state your terms?
3. Do you ensure that the customer's name, address and order number (if any) is correctly stated on your invoice?
4. Are your statements sent out promptly at the end of the month?
5. Are they clear and easy to follow? Would they make sense to you if you were the recipient?
6. Are you checking payments received against ledger entries?

Credit control

1. Does every account have a credit limit?
2. Is it based on first-hand knowledge of the customer as a credit risk or personally, his track record as a payer with you or others in your line of business, on representatives' reports or reliable trade references, or on bankers' references — in that order of usefulness?
3. Do you exercise special vigilance on new accounts?
4. Do your statements show the age of outstanding balances and do you or your credit controller look at outgoing statements to check on customers whose payments situation seems to be deteriorating?
5. Do you have a system for dealing with customers who exceed their credit limit?
6. Do you have a sequence of reminder procedures for dealing with overdue accounts by telephone calls and/ or letters?
7. Do you check orders received against a list of customers who have exceeded their credit limit or who are proving to be reluctant or non-payers?

8. Does the person in charge of credit control liaise with those responsible for supplying the account in question to make sure that there are no special reasons for non-payment before sharper warnings are delivered?

9. Do you regularly check on the debtor:sales ratio to make sure you are not heading for a liquidity problem by being too generous about extending credit?

6: Budgeting and Cash Flow Forecasting

One principle that it is vital to grasp is the importance of liquid cash in running a business. This should not be confused with profitability. Because of the way the profit figure is arrived at on the trading account (see Chapter 4), it is perfectly possible for a business to be trading profitably and yet be quite unable to pay the tax bill or the rent because its resources are tied up in stock or, even worse, in equipment.

Failure to understand the distinction between profit and cash flow is not uncommon and it can be disastrous. For instance, you may be offered very persuasive financial inducements to carry or manufacture additional stock. If it is a good product and one for which there is a consistent demand you may say to yourself that you are going to need more anyway in six months' time — so why not stock up for a whole year at a bargain price? This can be a valid argument, but before you accept it consider that when the bills come in they have to be paid with money, not with stock. Profitability means very little unless cash is there when it is needed.

This is true even for businesses that do not carry stocks, like a photographic studio producing goods only to order, or a design consultancy selling more or less intangible skills. You are still going to have outgoings on travel or materials; and even if your premises are a back room in your own house there are still rate demands to be met — apart from the little matter of needing money to live on.

Planning your cash requirements

Planning your cash requirements is most important, right from the outset of your career as a self-employed person. It will determine much of your policy towards what kinds of work you take on; far better, if you are short of liquid capital, to take on a number of small jobs which will keep money coming in than one big, tempting, potentially profitable one where you might run out of cash three-quarters of the way through. For unless you make provision to get progress payments from your customer backed up, possibly by a bank overdraft, your suppliers are going to be pressing you for payment before you are in a position to send your bills to the customer. Even at best, in most businesses which are not taking cash across the counter there is going to be a lag between the time you are being asked for payment and when your customer pays you.

In order to estimate what your needs for cash are going to be you should set up and revise at three- or six-monthly intervals, a cash flow budget; and in order to refine it, you should also check it back against what actually happened.

The words 'cash flow budget' sound intimidatingly technical, but all they amount to is that you should make a realistic forecast of money coming in and going out over the period. Again, how accurate you can be depends somewhat on the circumstances and the type of business you are in. If you have bought a going concern there may be regular contracts that you hope to maintain, or in the case of a retail business or a restaurant some kind of predictable pattern of trade which can be established from the cash book or general ledger. If you have started a new business of your own, on the other hand, you may not have much to go on in the way of facts on cash coming in. You might only have enough certain information on the next two or three months, though if you have asked yourself the questions we outlined in Chapter 1 you will have ensured, as far as possible, that there is a continuing demand for your product so that orders will go on arriving while you are completing the work you have already lined up. But even in cases where you don't know where the penny after next is coming from, at the very least the cash flow budget will tell you what commitments you have to meet, and therefore what volume of sales should be your target to this end. You can include this sales target in your budget — but don't forget that in order to achieve it costs of materials and additional overheads will also be involved; also, both in cases where income is firmly expected and where it is only a forecast of expectations the cost of materials and wages will have to be met before you actually get paid.

Let's take a hypothetical case here to illustrate a cash flow budget in operation over the first four months of the year for a small offset printing business with two partners and one employee. Over these months they have a contract to print the spring catalogue from a local firm of nurserymen, a monthly list from a firm selling militaria by mail order and a booklet on the town for the Chamber of Commerce. They also have some orders for what is known as 'jobbing' — small jobs such as wedding invitations, brochures, printed labels and the like — with the prospect that a regular flow of such work can be picked up. Against this, they have to meet wages, rent, PAYE, VAT, telephone, the running of a van and, of course, materials.

As you will see from the forecast, the partners budgeted for a deficit in the first two months, but they were not worried because they knew that in March and April they could expect a couple of big payments from Rosebud Nurseries and from the Chamber of Commerce. However, in order to keep solvent they had to borrow £2000 from the bank, interest payments on which had to be paid at intervals. Another thing they had to do was to plan the purchase of their most costly item — paper — as close as possible to the month in which they would actually be using it for their two big jobs. No point in holding expensive stock which can't be used at an early date. Even though, with inflation, it might actually have been cheaper for them to have ordered all their paper for the first four months back in January, their bank overdraft would not have been sufficient to meet the bill.

In March they had to allow for three quarterly items — electricity, telephone and their VAT return; and as the year progresses they will have to make plans to meet such major items as rates and taxes. Note also that expenditure which is central to the activities of the business — in this case paper — has to be forecast more carefully than incidentals such as postage where a monthly average has been extended. If postage was a more crucial factor, as might be the case with a mail-order firm, this part of the cash flow budget would have to be worked out in more detail.

Regarding the revenue part of the forecast, the partners had enough orders for jobbing work to budget fairly accurately for the first two months. For March and April they guessed a figure, hoping spring weddings and a general

	January	February	March	April
Income				
Source	From December Statement	From January Statement	From February Statement	From March Statement
	Militaria Ltd. £500	Militaria Ltd £500	Rosebud Nurseries Ltd £5300	Chamber of Commerce £2000
	Other work £400	Other work £250	Militaria Ltd £500	Militaria Ltd £500
			Other work £500	Other work £500
	£900	£750	£6300	£3000
Expenditure				
Wages, salaries, PAYE, National Insurance	£750	Wages, etc. £750	Wages, etc. £750	Wages, etc. £750
Rent	£100	Rent £100	Rent £100	Rent £100
Maintenance contract	£20	Maintenance £20	Maintenance £20	Maintenance £20
Petrol	£40	Petrol £40	Petrol £40	Petrol £40
Postage	£20	Postage £20	Postage £20	Postage £20
Travel and Entertainment	£40	Travel, etc. £40	Travel, etc. £40	Travel, etc. £40
Materials	£100	Materials £100	Materials £150	Materials £100
Bank Interest		£60		
Electricity			£70	
Telephone			£40	
VAT			£300	
Paper	£1500		£1000	£1500
Other materials	£200			
	£2670	£1130	£2530	£2570
Cash Surplus (Deficit)	(£1770)	(£380)	£3770	£430

Figure 8. *An example of a cash flow budget.*

upturn of business after the winter would lead to a modest growth in incoming funds after that point.

The overall March and April figures look quite rosy, but after that it was clear that they would have to turn up some more jobs like Rosebud Nurseries and the Chamber of Commerce booklet because the overheads — wages, rent, the maintenance contract on their machines, bank interest — plus the cost of paper and materials needed to fill forecast work were running slightly above the expected income. So even though they are running well ahead of the game at the end of April, they would be unwise to start reducing that bank overdraft just yet.

There are many other lessons to be learned from your cash flow budget — they vary from business to business — but the essential points are that it is an indispensable indicator in making your buying decisions both of stock and materials, that it helps you decide your priorities between getting work (and what sort of work) and devoting all your energies to executing it and points up the importance of getting the maximum credit — and allowing the minimum!

Checklist: budgeting and cash flow

1. Is the forecast of money coming in based on firm orders or at least reasonable expectations or does it include an element of fond hope?
2. Are the customers concerned likely to pay you at the times forcast?
3. Can you persuade any large customers to offer you progress payments to help you over difficult months?
4. Have you included everything in the outgoings section of the budget, including allowing for things like VAT and the heating of premises in winter months?
5. Do you have the resources to see you through deficit months, or have you secured finance to this end?
6. Is there any way you can cut down on the expenditure element by delaying or staggering buying decisions of stock or leasing rather than buying equipment?

7: Raising Money

In the previous chapter, when listing the ways in which your cash flow budget can help you plan the cash requirements of your business, we have touched in passing on the role of the bank as a source of funds. There are, of course, other methods of raising money which we shall discuss. Some of these are direct forms of borrowing or obtaining loans, others are ways in which you can spin out your cash resources. But for most small businesses — and many large ones — bank borrowing is the one most widely used.

Approaching your bank

Banks make money by using the funds deposited with them to lend out at rates of interest which vary according to government policy. During periods of economic expansion that rate will be lower — and money easier to get — than during the 'stop' parts of the 'stop and go cycle' which has characterised the British economy since the war. But banks, like everybody else, have to continue to trade even through less prosperous times. You will find, therefore, that the bank manager will be willing to discuss making money available to you, because potentially you are a source of income to him. How much that will be depends somewhat on the size of the branch you are approaching. This is an argument in favour of going to a large branch if you need a sizeable sum; on the other hand in a smaller community, where personal contacts still matter, your professional adviser may well have a shrewd idea of what the bank manager's lending limits are. But whether you can convince him that your business is a good risk depends on how well you have thought out your approach. To some extent he will go on personal impressions and on what he can gather of your previous business experience. Of course, if you have already been running your own firm for a year or two he will have some hard evidence to go on in the shape of your profit and loss account and your balance sheet. He will be looking at some of the ratios we talked about in Chapter 4, particularly the relationship of current assets to current liabilities and of debtors to creditors. He will want to be satisfied that you are valuing your stock realistically and he will want to know how much money you (and your partners, if you have any) have put into the business from your own resources. In the case of a limited company he will want to know what the issued share capital is. In other words he will be looking to see whether your business satisfies three criteria: firstly that his money is secure, and in the case of new business he will probably ask for security to be in the shape of tangible items like fixed assets within the business or shares and other assets belonging to the owners in their private capacity in a ratio which may be as high as 1:1. Secondly that your firm is likely to have an inflow of enough liquid assets to enable him to recall his money, if necessary; and thirdly that you will be able to make profitable use of it and pay the interest without difficulty.

There is a saying that banks will only lend you money if you don't need it and reading these requirements you may be coming to the conclusion that there is an element of truth in it! But what it really means is that it is no use going to a bank to bail you out of trouble. A business in trouble generally requires assistance on the management side at the very least and banks are just not in a position to provide such assistance, no matter how glowing the prospects might be if the firm could be brought back on track. So the bank manager is only going to be looking at present and quantifiable situations. He will not be very interested in often vague assets like goodwill and even less in your hopes for the future.

Of course, if you have only just set up in business you may not have much more than hopes for the future to offer, and the bank manager will obviously be cautious in such cases. But even these hopes can be quantified, and this is where your cash flow budget comes in. If you are opening, say, a new restaurant facts such as that you and your wife are excellent cooks, have attended courses in catering and have established that there would be a demand for a good place to eat in a particular locality are, of course, relevant. But what the bank also wants to know is what your start-up costs are going to be, whether you have fully worked out what your overheads and direct costs are (ie items like rent, rates, gas and electricity, depreciation on equipment, staff wages and the costs of food) what relation these are going to bear to your charges for meals, and what levels of seat occupancy you need to achieve to make a profit. This may take quite a lot of working out and it is advisable that you consult closely with your accountant in preparing your case for the bank. Indeed it is a good idea to take your accountant along with you when you are approaching the bank for financial help. Where larger sums are involved you may be required to have an independent cash flow assessment prepared.

The commonest form of help, as far as the small business is concerned, is an overdraft, rather than a bank loan. You will be given facilities to overdraw up to a certain amount, but the advantage of an overdraft, as opposed to a loan, is that interest (usually two per cent to three per cent above base lending rate) is paid only on the actual amount by which you are overdrawn. Overdrafts are particularly useful, therefore, for the firm whose pattern of business fluctuates, for instance, a market gardener whose income is higher in spring than in winter — or which needs money to finance a large contract until the first progress payments are received. The disadvantage of an overdraft is that it can be called in. Though in practice this rarely happens, it is unwise to use money raised in this way to finance medium and long-term requirements, particularly those which make no immediate contribution to profits — like having your office done up! A more likely peril than the overdraft being called in, however, is the fluctuation of interest rates. If these go up sharply because of some economic crisis, you want to be in a position where you are keeping the facility you are using down to a minimum.

If you do need to finance the cost of purchasing plant or equipment, however, you might sleep more easily if you have negotiated a bank loan. This would normally run for between two and five years, would have repayment periods built into it and would carry a somewhat higher rate of interest than an overdraft. Alternatively, you may need a mixed package — both overdraft facilities and a term loan. Your bank manager and your accountant should be able to advise you on your requirements, provided you have worked out a clear plan for the course of your business over the period during which you need financial help. For larger sums you might consider, with the help of your trusty financial adviser, an approach to the Industrial and Commercial Finance Corporation (ICFC). Its London office is at 91 Waterloo Road, London SE1 8XP, but it also has local offices in other cities. The advantage of ICFC is that although it is a commercial body (it was in fact founded by the clearing banks and the Bank of England), it is rather less aggressive than some of its competitors in its approach to participation in the equity and management of the companies to which it lends money; but it is not, on the whole, interested in getting involved in businesses that are not yet established — especially small ones.

In the case of a limited company, the bank is likely to call on individual directors to guarantee any overdrafts or loans against their personal resources. There are certain pitfalls about some forms of guarantee and it is vital that you check with your solicitor when entering into such an arrangement. If you find the terms under which your bank is offering finance unacceptable, it is worth shopping around to see if you can get a better deal elsewhere.

Private loans

You may have friends or relatives who are prepared to lend you money, but private loans are a rich source of misunderstanding, so you should be clear about all the implications of such an arrangement. The best plan is to get a solicitor to draw up the terms of the loan, covering the rate of interest, the period over which the loan is repayable and the circumstances under which it can be withdrawn. It must also be made clear to what extent, if any, the lender has any say in the running of the business and what the nature of this control is. Normally, however, the lender should not be entitled to participation in management matters; nor does the existence of his loan entitle him to a share of the profits — no matter how strong a moral claim he thinks he might have once your business starts making real money. In the case of a limited company, you must explain to the lender that a loan is not the same thing as a shareholding — though of course the offer of a loan might be conditional on acquiring shares or the option to acquire them. You should be clear about the implications of this — it entitles the shareholder to a percentage of profits in proportion to his holdings; and though loans can be repaid it is virtually impossible to dismantle issued share capital in this way.

Often private loans are not offered directly; but in the form of guaranteeing an overdraft on the basis that, if the recipient of the overdraft is unable to repay it, then the guarantor is liable for that amount. In the 1978 Budget an important concession was made in relation to such arrangements. Losses incurred by the guarantor of a business loan can now be treated as a capital loss, which can be offset against capital gains. This was not the case before.

It is possible, by the way, in the case of a limited company for the shareholders to lend money to the company. This does not increase their liability in the same way as taking up issued share capital. However, outside lenders like banks do not take kindly to such arrangements because it indicates a certain reluctance by the shareholders to put their money where their mouth is!

Money from the government

One of the problems of excessive government legislation is that it becomes increasingly difficult to sort out the useful bits from the others, so that there is a tendency to shove the whole lot to one side. This is certainly true of the Industry Act of 1972, which in fact includes provision for financial help to businesses, large and small. The government has millions of pounds available for this purpose, the money being offered in the form of cash grants and special rate loans. In particular, they are trying to promote industrial development in the so-called special development areas, which in the main are those areas where traditional industries, like shipbuilding, are on the decline and where unemployment is therefore apt to be high. The minimum project values go as low as £10,000-£50,000 and though the authorities tend to look more favourably at established businesses who are relocating in development areas, the prospects are certainly worth investigating if you are in or are thinking of moving to such an area. Development areas have the further advantage of usually having a large pool of local labour, and though the spectre of unemployment is no longer a guarantee for getting a cooperative labour force together, unions in such areas are often fairly realistic in their demands. Application forms for assistance in moving to a development area can be obtained from the Department of Industry, 1 Victoria Street, London

SW1.

If your proposed enterprise is in a small town or a rural area in England or Wales, you should have a word with the Council for Small Industries in Rural Areas: CoSIRA (Head Office: Queen's House, Fish Row, Salisbury, Wiltshire SP1 1EX, 0772-24411). As the name implies, they concentrate on industries — including tourism — and cannot offer assistance in the spheres of agriculture, horticulture or retail shops.

A number of similar regional bodies also exist: The Welsh Development Office, the Scottish Development Office, The Highlands and Islands Development Board, and the Northern Ireland Development Office. Your regional Small Firms Information Centre should be able to advise you whether you have a case for approaching them. Addresses are given in the back of this book.

But what about that marvellous invention that nobody will finance? Is the government prepared to put its money where its mouth is in sponsoring British initiatives in new technology? The answer is a guarded yes. There is such a body, but it is reputed to take an extremely cautious view of approaches made to it. Perhaps for this reason and because it demands a 50:50 share of the action if the idea works, it has been financially very successful. The body in question is the National Research Development Corporation, 66 Victoria Street, London SW1.

Finance houses and merchant banks

Despite the fact that many business success stories one reads about in the financial sections of the press begin with the owners getting a loan from a merchant bank, this is not usually a viable source of finance for the small business — ie one with a turnover of under £100,000. These banks are set up to finance fairly large-scale operations and they do not usually wish to get involved with smaller firms, even if they are profitable and soundly run.

If you do feel that your firm offers the opportunity for rapid growth to the sort of scale that would interest a merchant bank, it will of course be worth your while talking to them. But your case will have to be very soundly prepared indeed, they will almost certainly want a substantial share in the equity and their interest charges must not be forgotten. They will be as high as the going market rate.

High interest rates are also a characteristic of hire-purchase arrangements made with the help of a finance company. This is a useful way of financing medium to longer term commitments, like the purchase of machinery, equipment and vehicles. The arrangements are basically similar to a private hire-purchase contract, in that the buyer asks the finance company to buy the asset. He then hires it for a specific period, paying hiring charges and interest as he goes along; and can then exercise an option to buy goods at the end of an agreed period. Until that point they remain the property of the finance company, and there is thus no need, as a rule, for the hirer to provide security as is the case with a loan. On the other hand, the finance company will require him to maintain the asset in good order, to insure it and possibly to fulfil other special conditions like providing satisfactory evidence that the money earned from it will at least cover the high interest charges (around 20 per cent at present) involved.

The periods over which a hire-purchase agreement may run vary with the nature of the asset, but in general terms the Finance Houses Association lays down that 'the goods should have a useful life greater than the period of the hire purchase agreement'.

Using your own money

Inevitably you will have to put up at least some money of your own. Even if your form of business involves selling an intangible skill, as in the case of consultancy, you are going to need some basic equipment — not to mention the fact that you have to have enough money to live on until your business income builds up. You should bear in mind that any money of your own that you put into your firm should be earning a rate of interest comparable to what you could get outside, and this must be reflected in your costing and estimating, a topic that is dealt with in more detail in Chapter 8.

Apart from ready cash in the form of savings, jewellery and other liquid and saleable personal assets you will also have other, less immediate resources to turn to. The most obvious is your house and if you bought it before the huge rise in property prices which took place in the early seventies its current value may be far in excess of your mortgage. You could take out a second mortgage on this basis, but interest rates on second mortgages are very high. A better approach would be to take out a mortgage on another house and sell the one you are in.

Life insurance policies are also worth bearing in mind because companies will generally be prepared to lend money against up to 90 per cent of their surrender value. Whether this yields a worthwhile amount of cash obviously varies from case to case. Interest rates on these loans, however, are generally less than on bank overdrafts.

Raising money by effective cash management

Any method of raising money from the outside costs money. In a period of high interest rates, borrowing can be so costly as to swallow up the entire profits of a business that is over-reliant on it. There are, of course, instances where borrowing huge amounts of money has made sense — for instance in the property market, where the value of assets has (until recently) increased much faster than the value of the money borrowed to acquire them. But recent events have shown that this is dependent on the assumption that the asset does go on appreciating in value at a very rapid rate, and certainly from the point of view of the smaller business one could state as golden rules the following: never borrow more than you have to, never buy until you need to. And when you need to, consider whether hire purchase or even leasing might not make more sense for you than committing cash to an outright purchase. Remember it is cash that pays the bills — not assets, nor paper profits.

A surprising amount of borrowing can be avoided by effective cash management. It is not dishonest to take the maximum period of payment allowed by your suppliers, and though you don't want to get the reputation of being a slow payer once you have established a reputation of being a reliable account your suppliers may give you quite a bit of leeway before they start pressing you for payment even on an overdue sum. Nor is it dishonest to take note that some suppliers press for payment fairly quickly, whereas others are more lax. The former get paid first.

The reverse is true in the case of the customers you supply. Send out invoices as soon as the work is done. You are more likely to get paid at that point than some weeks later when the novelty has worn off and maybe quibbles have arisen.

Send out statements punctually and make sure that your terms of payment are observed.

Progress payments

In the case of work done on contract — say a design or consultancy job involving sizeable sums of money over a longer period of time like three or four months — it is worth trying to persuade your customer to make advance and/or progress payments. After all, you are going to be involved in considerable expenditure before the final sum becomes due. Whether an approach of this kind should be made depends of course on how well you know the customer and how badly you think he needs you. If you need his work more than he needs your services, you should consider a bank overdraft, though the cost of this should be reflected in your charges.

Credit Factoring

Credit management is a tricky business which has sunk more than one promising new enterprise which, hungry for business, too inexperienced or simply too busy to pay attention to time-consuming detail, has let its credit index — the length of time money is outstanding — get out of control. A possible solution is to get a credit factor to look after this aspect for you. The way they operate is that the firm using their services continues to send out its own invoices but the factor — who, of course, gets copies of the invoices — takes over the whole business of collecting the receivables. He will also generally give advice on credit limits and, if required to do so, may be able to discount the invoices — ie allow you to draw cash from him against a percentage of the amounts he is due to collect. Naturally they charge a fairly substantial fee for this service, varying with turnover, and on the whole they are not interested in firms whose turnover is less than £100,000 pa nor in those invoicing too many small amounts to small customers. Your bank or local Chamber of Commerce should be able to advise you on the choice of a factor. Indeed a number of banks have subsidiaries who offer a factoring service. There is also now an Association of British Factors, made up of some of the largest firms in the business.

Checklist: raising money

1. How much do you need?
2. Is it to finance short or long-term financial facilities?
3. Should you be looking to your bank for overdraft facilities? If so, to what limit?
4. Should you be looking for a term loan from your bank or some other commercial or official body? If so, how much and over what period?
5. Have you considered leasing or hire purchase as an alternative to raising a lump sum? If this option is open to you, have you worked out the cost of leasing and HP finance as compared to interest charges on loans?
6. If your need for cash is related to difficulties with credit control, have you considered invoice factoring?
7. Have you considered liquidating personal assets to raise cash?
8. Assuming options 5, 6 and 7 have been considered and rejected, have you worked out how to repay the loan and interest charges?
9. What security can you offer a lender, and has it been independently valued?
10. Exactly how do you propose to use the money?
11. Have you prepared a written description of your firm, what skills the key people in it have to offer, what your objectives are, how your product or service compares with the competition, what firm orders you have secured and what your realistic expectations, opportunities and goals are?
12. Do you have supporting evidence on orders you have obtained or are likely to obtain?
13. Have you (and your associates, if any) made as full a commitment to your enterprise in terms of time and money as can reasonably be expected of you?
14. Have you previously obtained financial help for this or any other business? Have you repaid it within the period due?
15. If you have any loans outstanding on the business, how much are they for, for what purpose and how are they secured?
16. Can you produce an up-to-date balance sheet showing the present financial state of your company?
17. Do you have a detailed cash flow projection, monthly

over the first two years and quarterly thereafter, showing cash flow over the period of the loan?

18. Do you have annual projected profit and loss accounts and balance sheets over the period of the loan?

19. If you are approaching a merchant bank or private individual for venture capital have you considered how much of the equity in and control of your company you are prepared to let go?

20. If you are raising money to enable you to fulfil a large contract have you talked to your customer about the possibility of his paying you in stages?

8: Costing, Pricing and Estimating

How much should you charge your customers? Or, to put it more searchingly, on what factors should your charges be based? It is surprising that many self-employed people would be hard put to it to give a clear answer to that question. Of course, there are such things as 'going rates' and 'recommended' (or generally accepted) prices, but often these are in the nature of broad guidelines and unless you know what all your costs are — not just the cost of materials, or how long the job took you — you are sooner or later going to be in the position of either undercharging or making an actual loss.

Of course, there are some self-employed occupations where the scope for how much you can charge is either narrow or non-existent. This applies particularly to many areas of the retail trade, where goods tend to have recommended prices printed on them by the suppliers; but even there you may want to consider *reducing* some prices in order to undercut a competitor and the question arises whether you can afford to do so. This depends on your overall costs — rent, rates, power supplies and many other factors. Equally, some freelance jobs are subject to generally accepted 'going rates' and the more commonplace such jobs are — the smaller the degree of service or expertise that is involved — the more strictly you have to keep within that rate. But the corollary of this statement is also true: the more unique your product or service, the more you can afford to charge for it.

This can apply even in the ordinary retail trade where, on the face of things, the prospect of getting away with charging more than the competition is not promising. Recently an East African Asian immigrant opened a small supermarket near my house. He is open late at night, on Sundays and on public holidays. Quite rightly, he charges for that extra time — most things cost a penny or two above what they do in the big shops down the High Street — but he is offering something more than they are. His way of meeting competition is not to charge less, but to provide more — a much-needed neighbourhood service for out-of-hours shopping.

The same principle can be applied to even rather routine freelance jobs. Provide a straightforward typing service and you will have to stick pretty much to the going rate; but offer something special, like accurately typing mathematical material or unusually high turnround speeds and you can move into a different price bracket.

Determining your costs

You could say to yourself: 'I'm going to charge as much as I can get away with' or, 'I'm going to charge the standard rate for the job'. These are quite sensible guidelines to be going on with, but at some point you are probably going to be in the situation of wondering whether you should be charging a little bit more; or perhaps whether you can afford to shave your price in order to land some work that you badly want. It is then that you have to get to grips with what your costs really are.

The most obvious one is your own time, and curiously enough it is an element that self-employed people are often confused about, because they tend to regard it as being somehow different from the time taken by employees. If a job involves your working flat out for a 100-hour week, you are underpricing the product of that work if your remuneration is less than that of an employed person doing the same kind of work at full overtime rates. There may, of course, be a reason why you *should* be undercharging: you may want a 'loss-leader' introduction to a particular customer, or to undercut a competitor — or you may simply need the money that week. But if you undercharge, you should be clear in your mind why you are doing so.

Another factor that is sometimes overlooked is that in most cases there are overhead costs incurred in running your business, irrespective of whether you have work coming in or not. We will deal with these overheads in more detail in a moment, but the point to be made here is to correct any misconception that the margin between what you charge and your basic costs in time and/or materials represents your profit. True, it is profit of a kind — gross profit. But the real profit element in a job, the net profit, only emerges when the overhead costs have been met. So the right way to work out your price to the customer — or to determine whether a job is worth taking on — is to establish whether it will pay for materials, overheads, wages (if you employ others) and still leave you with a margin of net profit that adequately reflects the time and skill you are putting into it.

Once you have been in business for a few months you should have accumulated enough facts and figures to establish what your overhead costs are. To what extent you can control the situation beyond that depends, again, on what sort of business you are in. If you are running an ordinary retail shop, operating on margins that are more or less fixed by the supplier, there is not much you can do about pricing your goods, but at least you will know whether you can afford to spend more on extra fittings or take on more staff — or whether you should be staying open longer to attract extra trade. But if you are manufacturing something, then you can work out a rule-of-thumb method in the form of a percentage to add on to your materials costs in quoting prices; or in the case of a service, an average hourly rate. It is important, though, to keep on monitoring these rule-of-thumb procedures against what actually happened, so you should keep a record detailing the specification of each job, in which actual costs can be compared against your original estimate. Over a period of time you should in this way be able to build up a reliable set of costs which can be referred to when a similar-sounding assignment comes up.

At the beginning, though, you will have very little to go on, so let us look in more detail at the factors you will have to take into account:

Costs connected with your premises Rent, heat, light, telephone, rates, insurance, finance (if you own or have bought a lease of the premises), cleaning and maintenance contracts.

Costs of finance Interest charged on overdrafts or loans. You should include in this calculation interest on any money you yourself have put into the business, because it should be earning a rate of return equivalent to what you could get on the open market.

Costs of equipment If you are renting equipment or buying

it on hire purchase this item of expenditure presents no problems. The issue is more complicated if you have bought equipment outright, because you have to figure out some way of recovering the purchase price and his is done by bringing in the concept of 'depreciation'. What this means is that you gradually write off, over a period of time based on the item's useful life, most of the amount you paid initially; not all, because it will have some resale value at the end of the depreciation period.

Supposing you bought a van for £3000 and you think it will last you for four years, at the end of which time you could expect to get £1000 for it. This leaves you with £2000 to depreciate over four years — £500 per annum. There are also a number of other ways to calculate depreciation and your accountant will advise you on the method most advantageous to your kind of business. The important point to bear in mind, though, is that depreciation is a real factor, not just an accountancy device. Assets like motor cars and equipment do wear out and have to be replaced. Reserves should be built up to enable you to do this.

Administrative costs Running your business will involve general expenditure which cannot be directly related to particular assignments: stationery, publicity, travel, postage, entertainment of clients, fees to professional advisers, and so forth.

Salaries and welfare Salaries are best calculated as an hourly rate, based on an average working week. In the case of employees these rates are usually determined by the market for that particular kind of employment. The problem is deciding how much you should pay to yourself. Again, this obviously varies with the kind of business you are in, but as a rough guideline you should, after meeting all your expenses, be earning at least as much as an employed person with the same degree of skill and responsibility. It is most important to cost your time properly; let us, therefore, look at a worked example of what might be involved in the case of a person in full-time self-employment.

Supposing you were aiming to earn £6000 a year. To start with you would want to take into account four weeks' annual paid holiday (three weeks, plus statutory holidays) and you would assume an eight-hour day and a five-day working week. However, not all your time would be directly productive: some of it would be spent travelling, on administration and on getting work. So let us say your productive time is 32 hours a week. That would give you an hourly rate based on 32 x 48 hours a year: 1536 hours. Divided into £4000 that means a rate of approximately £3.90 per hour. On top of that you have to allow for welfare items: your national insurance stamp, possibly contributions to a retirement pension scheme and certainly insurance against sickness or death. Let's assume this comes to another £600 a year. Divided by 1536 working hours, this adds another 39 pence to your hourly rate.

Similarly, when costing the time of any full-time staff working for you, it is not just a question of calculating basic rates of pay. You have to allow for holidays, the employer's contribution to national insurance stamps and to the graduated pension scheme. These items can add from six to eight per cent to the cost of wages.

Variable costs All the costs we have just described are fixed costs. You incur them whether you have work coming in or not. Variable costs are items like materials which can be attributed to specific jobs. Of course, there are circumstances in which what we have described as fixed costs can vary slightly. If you are running a lot of overtime, this will mean an increase in your fuel bills and extra payments to your staff or to yourself. But the benefit of achieving properly costed increases in productivity — for instance, in the case of a shop staying open late to attract more trade — is that, provided you are able to keep fixed overheads stable, this element will form a smaller proportion relative to your turnover; and that means a more profitable business.

Establishing your prices

You now have a set of basic data on costs which can be applied to your prices when you are asked to quote for a job or in making up your invoice. If you are supplying a service, the best way to do this is to take all your fixed costs, establish an hourly rate based on your usual working week and then estimate how long the job will take you. The effect of this is, of course, that if jobs do not materialise in the way the 'usual working week' concept implies you yourself are going to be carrying the can for the fixed overheads which are being incurred during all the hours in that week when you are not working; but if you only get 20 hours' work during a week in which you had budgeted for 40, loading your charges to the customer to make up for the shortfall could mean that you will come up with an unacceptable quotation or a price that will discourage your customer in the future.

The other lesson to be learned is that fixed overheads should be kept as low as possible. For instance, if you are planning a freelance design service to earn extra money in the evenings you should be chary of acquiring expensive equipment. In the limited hours of work which a spare-time freelance operation implies you may never be able to charge enough money to do more than pay the overheads. As far as possible, keep your costs in the variable category by hiring or renting equipment only when and for as long as you need it.

This is also true of businesses that produce manufactured articles (and activities which operate on lines similar to manufacturing like a restaurant, where the product is created in the form of a meal); though in these cases some machinery and equipment is usually essential. The price here will be based on a unit per item rather than on an hourly rate, but the principle is the same. Instead of fixing an hourly rate based on an expected working week, calculations should be made on a projected volume of costs spread over the number of units sold. Thus, if you aimed to sell in a week 20 chairs which cost you £3 each in materials your variable costs would be £60. If your fixed overheads, including your own remuneration, came to £100 a week, you would have to charge £8 per chair; and do not forget that even if your object is only to make a living wage out of your business, you should still be putting aside reserves to replace equipment as it wears out — and that the cost of doing so will, in inflationary times, be a great deal higher than its original cost.

Preparing quotations

With many jobs, whether they are a service or a commission to manufacture something, you will be asked to supply a quotation before a firm order is placed. Once that quotation has been accepted it is legally binding on both parties, so it is important not only to get your sums right but to make it clear in the wording attached to them what exactly you are providing for the money. In the case of a decorating job, for instance, you should specify who is providing the materials and, if you are, to what standards they are going to be.

Consider also whether any out-of-pocket expenses will be involved (travel, subsistence) and whether these are to be met by your customer or whether they have been allowed for in your quotation.

Apart from variable factors such as these, every quotation should set out the conditions of sale under which it is being offered. Different businesses will involve different kinds of conditions, but here are some basic points to bear in mind:

1. Particularly in times of inflation, you should make it clear that the prices quoted are current ones and may have to go up if costs rise during the course of the job.
2. Terms of payment should be set out — eg net 30 days.
3. You will have to cover the not uncommon situation of the customer changing his mind about the way he wants the job done subsequent to his accepting your quotation. You should leave yourself free to charge extra in such circumstances.
4. If you have agreed to complete a job within a certain length of time, set out the factors beyond your control which would prevent you from meeting the agreed date.
5. You should make it clear what circumstances of error, loss or damage will be your responsibility and what would fall outside it.
6. You should stipulate that, once the quotation is accepted, the order cannot be cancelled except by mutual consent and that the customer will be liable for all charges up to that point.
7. You should mention that the total is subject to VAT at the date ruling at the date of invoice. This is particularly important when the customer is a private person who is unable to claim back his VAT inputs. (See Chapter 10 for more details of VAT.)

Having gone to all the trouble to set out the quotation and conditions of sale, you should not neglect to check, before you start work, that the customer has actually accepted it in writing! It is all too easy to forget this or to imagine that an amicable verbal OK is sufficient. If a dispute arises, however, you will be very thankful to have carried out all the formal steps of documentation.

Checklist: costing, pricing and estimating

1. How unique is your product or service? If it is not particularly unique, how can you make it more so?
2. How essential is it to the customer?
3. What is the competition charging for the same or similar product or service?
4. How badly do you need the job or order?
5. Is your customer likely to come back for more if the price is right, or is it a one-off?
6. Will doing business with this customer enable you to break into a wider market, and thus enable you to reduce your unit costs?
7. What is the element of risk involved (ie is the customer, to your knowledge, a quick and certain payer)?
8. Do you have any idea how long the job will take you?
9. Can you relate the time element to your fixed costs?
10. Have you made a full assessment of all your fixed costs?
11. Do you have any idea what your materials are going to cost you?
12. Have you costed your own time properly?
13. Will the job leave you a margin of net profit? Or should you forego this in the interest of meeting fixed costs?
14. Have you prepared a quote, specifying exactly what you are going to provide or do, including terms of payment?
15. Has the customer accepted your quotation?
16. Are you keeping records of what the job cost you so that you can adjust your prices or quote more accurately next time?

9: Marketing Your Work

Good ideas, it is sometimes dismissively said, are 10 a penny; the implication being that the really difficult part is putting them into effect. Apart from the obvious virtues of persistence, hard work and technical know-how, this also requires a modicum of marketing skill. In other words, you will have to know whether there is a big enough demand for your product or service at the price you need to charge to make a living; and you will have to know how to identify and reach your potential customers.

Manufacturers

You may be the world's most skilful maker of hand-carved, model sailing ships, but unless enough people want hand-carved, model sailing ships you are going to have a hard time trying to make a living out of producing them commercially. So before you start in business, look around. Go to gift shops, luxury stores or wherever it is that the kind of item you are aiming to produce is being sold and find out about prices, quality standards and the extent of the demand. Any intelligent shop manager or assistant will be glad to give you such information, provided you don't buttonhole them at a busy time of the day — particularly as they're probably in that department because they are basically interested in that kind of product. It may be that by modifying your idea in quite a minor way, you will come up with a much more saleable article than the one that was originally in your mind.

Another point to watch out for is whether there is a long-term future for your product. This is particularly true with regard to fashion goods. There may be a craze for some particular kind of accessory and for a while you will be able to sell everything you produce. But before long some big manufacturer will come along and make the same thing much more cheaply and distribute it more effectively than you can. When the craze dies down he will get off the bandwaggon and on to something else. Are you going to be able to keep a step ahead of him by being in a position to meet the next craze before the big manufacturers become aware of it?

You also have to keep an eye on competitors of your own size. If you are making and selling pottery, consider how many other craft potters are active in your area and whether your work is so good and so competitively priced that it doesn't matter how many there are; or whether you can produce something commercially viable that they are not doing.

But no matter how good or unique your product may be, the ultimate key to success lies in effective sales and distribution. At the smallest level you might be selling direct to the public through your own shop, as is the case with many craft goods, but you have to bear in mind that you need to achieve a considerable turnover for a shop in a good location to be viable. This is difficult if the range of specialisation is very narrow, and many small-scale manufacturers therefore combine having their own shop with direct mail and mail order (which we shall come to in a moment) and with marketing to other retail outlets. Shop and workshop premises can be combined within the same floor area, so that you can switch readily from the sales counter to the workbench when the shop is empty; but this requires permission from the local planning authority if a 'change of use' of what were originally shop premises is involved.

Starting-up costs will eat deeply into your capital, so unless you have enough experience of the marketing (as opposed to the manufacturing) end of your specialty to be absolutely convinced that you can sell it, it is a good idea to begin by making a few prototypes of the product and its packaging and by trying to get orders from retailers. The point is that though your friends and family may think your idea is wonderful, the acid test is whether it will survive in the marketplace. In the course of investigating this the natural conservatism of most branches of the retail trade may at times depress or irritate you, but it is worth listening to what people who are involved in it have to say. If the same criticisms keep on cropping up you should think seriously of modifying your prototype to take them into account.

Distribution can be another big headache and your premises should be big enough to enable you to hold roughly as many days' or weeks' supply of stock as it takes to replace it at its rate of demand. (That is, if a business is selling 10 chairs a week and it takes two weeks to get that number of replacements there should, ideally, be space for something like 20 chairs. A customer might be prepared to wait a week for delivery, but he is unlikely to wait a month.)

Accessibility of non-selling areas is important too. Adequate entry for goods and materials at the rear or side of the premises is often essential and will always save time and energy.

Shops and service industries

The first large shopping centre built in Britain was a flop because, among other disadvantages, it had no parking facilities and was situated in a working-class area a few minutes' walk away from a large, long-established and very popular street market. The developers, for all their vast financial resources, had ignored hotel magnate Conrad Hilton's three rules for siting a business serving the public: location, location and location. If you are thinking of setting up a shop, restaurant or some other service outlet, find out as much as possible about the area. What sort of people live there? Is the area declining economically or on the up and up? What is the range of competitors? How efficient do they look and how well are they doing? If you are thinking of opening a high-class restaurant and there are nothing but fish and chip establishments in the neighbourhood, does this mean that there is no demand for a good restaurant or a crying need for one?

Taking an analogous case — that of a bookshop — you would want to conduct some rule-of-thumb market research about the area before going any further. For instance, you would want to know whether there were enough people in the area to support such a venture, whether they were the sort of people (broadly speaking, middle-class) who regularly bought books, and how good the local library was. You would also want to know what impact the result of your market investigations might have on your trading policies. Thus, if there were a lot of families with young children around, you should be considering getting to know, and stocking, children's books; or, if there were a lot of students in the neighbourhood, it would be worth your while finding out what textbooks were being used in any local institutes of higher education.

The same broad principles apply to almost every kind of retail or service outlet and you will have to conduct this kind of research — which is really just plain commonsense — whatever your venture. Do not be tempted to overlook it just because you are buying what is supposed to be a 'going concern'. One reason why it is up for sale may be that, despite the owner's or agent's protestations to the contrary, it was doing badly. If that was because the previous owner was a poor manager or stocked the wrong kind of goods for the neighbourhood, you might be able to turn the business around; but if there was simply too much competition in the area from similar shops and there is no chance of trading viably in something else from the same address, you would be well advised to forget about those premises — however good a buy they may seem from a purely cost point of view. Of course, you will also be able to check on the vendor's assertions by looking, preferably with your accountant, at his profit and loss accounts — not just the past year's, but the previous three to five years', to get a picture of the general trend of things. On the whole, buying a going concern has to be approached with great caution, particularly by the inexperienced, because of the difficulties of valuing stock and goodwill with any accuracy.

Freelance services

Most freelances agree that the way you get work is by knowing people who are in a position to give it to you. That sounds rather like a chicken and egg situation, and to begin with, so it is. You would be ill-advised to launch into freelance work, certainly on a full-time basis, until you have built up a range of contacts who can provide you with enough work to produce some sort of living for at least the first few months. Often these are people whom you have got to know in the course of a full-time job, or while doing temporary work. Many advertising agencies, for instance, have been started by a breakaway group taking a batch of clients with them when they start up. And it may even be that your employer, having been compelled to make you redundant, will still be willing to put work out to you on a freelance basis.

Once you have got going and established a reputation for doing good, reliable work, things get much easier. For one thing, word-of-mouth recommendations have a strong effect in the freelance world; and for another, you will be able to produce examples of work sold, or be able to refer prospects to other clients who have engaged you successfully. Evidence, for instance, that your fashion photographs have actually been used by national magazines generally impresses more than a folder of prints, no matter how good they are. In freelance work, as in other spheres, nothing succeeds like success.

One problem with freelance work, though, is that clients often want something done in a hurry — over a weekend or even overnight. This can be highly inconvenient at times, but it is generally a bad idea to turn work down simply for this reason. If you have to be selective, turn away the smaller, less remunerative jobs or commissions from people who are slow to pay their bills. One thing you should never do, though, is to let a client down. If you cannot, or do not want to take on an assignment, say so right away.

Press advertising

Advertising is a marketing tool and like any other tool you have to use it in the right place, at the right time and for the right job if it is going to be of any use to you. For instance, if you are a local building contractor, there is no point advertising in national newspapers, because most of the circulation, which is what you are paying for in the rates charged, will be outside the geographical area you are working in. On the other hand, if you are making a product to sell by mail order, then the bigger the circulation the better — though even there, there are provisos; no point in advertising a product aimed at top people in a mass-circulation tabloid.

So the first rule is to pick the right medium for the product or service you have to sell. Do not be dazzled by circulation figures. What matters is the *quality* of the circulation in relation to your marketing needs, and a trade or local paper may often provide the best value for money.

A few years ago the writer of this chapter was responsible for marketing a very expensive American book on Japanese flower arranging. It turned out that there was a small journal with a circulation of a few hundred copies to devotees of this arcane hobby and a full-page advertisement (which then cost a mere £15), combined with an order coupon, produced a quite extraordinary response.

Of course, full-page advertisements normally cost a good deal more than that and in the nationals they can run to thousands of pounds. A small, regular insertion in a local or specialist paper is what you should be thinking of; and the keyword is 'regular'. People's needs change from week to week, and unless you happen to hit them in the week they need your product, you will not hit them at all.

Regular advertising need not be expensive. An advertisement in the 'classified' section (but be sure to specify the right classification!) costs only a few pounds, and there may be bulk rates for regular insertions.

You can also have a display advertisement. These are charged by column inches (or centimetres) rather than by line as is the case with classified. It costs more, but the advantage is that you may be able to control the position in which your advertisement is to appear. The top and outside edges are more eye-catching than, say, the inside corners. 'Facing matter' advertisements, particularly when they are facing a feature article relating to your kind of product, can also be very effective. It is a good idea to get a graphic designer — you will find plenty of addresses in Yellow Pages — to do a lay-out for you. It will only cost you a few pounds and the result will be infinitely more attractive and eye-catching than if you leave it to the printer's typesetter.

Some days are reckoned by admen to produce a better response than others, although there are divided opinions on what these days are. The best advice is to experiment with different days. It is worth experimenting with the wording, too. Try several variations on the same theme and use the one that brings you the best response. But avoid trying to cram in too many words. People do not, on the whole, respond to overcrowded ads.

One important feature is that your advertisment should be very specific about how the goods and services advertised can be obtained. Your address should be prominent and if you are only available at certain times of the day or in the evenings this should be stated. If you are selling a product, an order coupon (stating price *and* postage) reinforces this point. It will also enable you to measure the extent of the response. You should, in fact, keep a close eye on where most of your sales or assignments are coming from: the type of customer and how he is getting to hear about you. This will enable you to concentrate future marketing efforts in the most rewarding sectors.

Direct mail

Direct mail selling is a considerable subject in its own right. It differs from mail order in that the latter consists of mailing goods direct to the customer from orders engendered by general press advertising, whereas in the case of direct mail selling the advertising is a brochure or sales letter specifically directed at the customer; in most cases by name, though inserts in specialist journals are also a form of direct mail. Except in the latter case, this means you will have to allow for postage in your pricing and since the response to direct mail averages around two per cent, the postage cost per sale is quite a considerable factor. It can, however, be a very effective way of selling specialised, high-priced items (£8 is around the viable minimum these days) or of identifying people who are likely to buy from you regularly if you are selling variations on the same product — something like antique tools, for instance. But unless you are very skilful at writing brochures or sales letters you should get this done for you by an expert. Such people are employed by mailing list brokers (you will find those in the Yellow Pages) who will often provide a complete package — they will sell to you, or compile for you, specialised lists, address and stuff envelopes and produce sales literature.

Obviously such services are not cheap and before you plunge into a direct mail campaign there are relatively inexpensive ways of testing the market for yourself. Pick 100 specialist addresses of the type you want to reach on a bigger scale — again, you may find them in the Yellow Pages. (A small want ad in one of the advertising industry's trade papers will soon raise the services of freelance copywriters and designers if you need such help.) From the percentage reply to the sample mailing you will be able to gauge whether a bigger campaign is worth mounting and you will also get some idea of how to price the product to take into account the likely mailing costs per sale. It is generally essential, by the way, with direct mail advertising, to include a reply-paid card or envelope with your sales literature. Details of how to apply for reply-paid facilities are available from the Post Office.

Checklist: marketing your work

Manufacturers

1. Have you tested your idea by discussing your proposed product with potential customers? Or, better still, showing it to them?
2. Is the market for it big enough? How accessible is it?
3. Can the customers you have in mind afford a price that will produce a profit for you?
4. Have you studied the competition from the point of view of price, design quality, reliability, delivery dates etc?
5. Should you modify your produce in some way so as to get the edge on the competition? Have you worked out what this will do to your costs?
6. Is there a long-term future for your product? If not, do you have any ideas for a follow-up?
7. Can you handle distribution? Do you have access to a van if the market is local? Do you have adequate parking facilities if it requires despatching?
8. In the latter case, have you taken post and packing costs into account in working out how much the product will cost the customer?
9. Do you have adequate space to hold stock, taking into account production time?
10. Do you have someone who can deal with customer queries and complaints? Or have you allowed for the fact that you will have to take time out yourself to deal with them?

Shops and service industries

1. How much do you know about the area?
2. Is the location good from the point of view of attracting the kind of trade you are looking for?
3. What competitors do you have?
4. How are they doing?
5. Based on your study of the area, and the people who live in it, how does this affect the type of goods or the nature of the service you are going to offer?
6. If you are buying a going concern, have you checked it out thoroughly with your professional advisers?

Freelance services

1. Do you have any contacts who can give you work?
2. Have you made a realistic appraisal of how much you can expect to earn over the first six months?
3. Have you allowed for the fact that you will need a good deal of spare time to go around looking for more business?
4. What evidence can you produce of your competence to do freelance work in your proposed field?
5. Have you shown that evidence to the sort of person who might be a customer to get his reaction on whether it is likely to impress?
6. Who are your competitors, what do they charge and what can you offer that is superior to their services?

Advertising and promotion

1. Have you chosen the right medium to promote your product or service?
2. Do you have any idea of the circulation and how this is broken down, geographically or by type of reader?
3. Have you worked out any way of monitoring results, for instance by including a coupon?
4. Have you included the cost of advertising and promotion in your cash flow budget and in costing your product?
5. Have you worked out how many orders you need to get from your advertising/promotion campaign to show a profit?
6. In the case of a display advertisement, have you specified a position in which it is to appear?
7. Again, in the case of a display ad or a brochure have you had it properly designed?
8. Does your advertising/promotion material state where your product or service can be obtained and, if relevant, the price?
9. Is the wording compelling? Does it clearly describe the product or service and does it motivate the customer? Would you buy it, if you were a customer?
10. In the case of a classified advertisement, have you specified under which classification it is to appear?
11. Are all the statements and claims you are making about your product or service true to the best of your know-

ledge and belief, bearing in mind that untruths can leave you open to prosecution under the Trade Descriptions Act?

10: Taxation

How you are affected by taxation depends on the nature of the commercial activity in which you are engaged. Virtually everyone, of course, pays tax on income from some source, whether this be from full-time employment, from dividends or interest or from self-employment or from a combination of several of these elements. The various kinds of income are assessed under several headings or schedules and the ones we will be particularly concerned with are:

1. Schedule D. Case I and Case II: Income from trades, professions or vocations. (In the interests of simplicity we will refer to this as Schedule D, though there are four other 'Cases' of Schedule D income.)
2. Schedule E: Wages and salaries from employment.

There are also other ways in which you may be involved in tax matters. You may be paying capital gains tax on the disposal of capital assets. If you are employing people full-time, you will be responsible for administering their PAYE payments; also, in certain circumstances, your own PAYE. If you are a shareholder in a limited company, it will be paying corporation tax on its profits. Lastly, you may — and if your turnover exceeds £10,000 a year, you must — for the supply of certain goods and services collect VAT from your customers and pay it over to Customs and Excise, less any VAT on goods and services supplied to you in the course of business.

One cannot, in a book of this nature, deal with a subject as complex as taxation exhaustively. But with this proviso, let us look in broad outline at some of its principal implications.

Income tax

There are certain income-tax advantages in working for yourself, or even in earning a supplementary income from part-time self-employment. To some extent these advantages were eroded by the National Insurance contributions for the self-employed which came into force in April 1975 and imposed what was, in effect, an additional eight per cent tax on self-employed people's taxable income between £1600 and £3600 a year. In the 1978 Budget, though, this burden was somewhat lightened. For one thing the levy is now only payable by men under 65 and women under 60; more important, the rate has been reduced to five per cent on taxable earnings between £2000 and £6250 a year.

There has also been some reduction in the flat-rate weekly National Insurance contribution additionally payable by people who have an income from self-employment as well as a salary from another source. The earnings rate from self-employment above which this additional contribution has to be paid has been raised from £875 to £950 a year and the weekly contributions have been reduced from £2.60 for men and £2.55 for women respectively to £1.90 in both cases. There is, however, a maximum on the total contributions due and if your contributions exceed that maximum then the excess is refunded. Alternatively you can apply to defer your weekly contribution until the end of the year when your total potential contribution is known. Your accountant should be able to advise you on the best course of action to take. Details of what you have to do to get deferment is given in a government leaflet, NP 18.

The reasoning behind what remains a somewhat doctrinaire piece of legislation appears to be that self-employed people are obtaining tax concessions that are not offered to the rest of the community. There is therefore a correspondingly strong case for taking the fullest possible advantage of these concessions in so far as they are indeed available.

Like the income of employed persons, the income from self-employment in its various forms is subject to an ascending rate of tax, ranging from 34 per cent (and actually only 25 per cent in the first £750 of income) to 83 per cent; subject, that is, to certain personal tax reliefs (eg allowances for dependent relatives, for part of the premiums on life assurance policies etc) which you can deduct from your total income in arriving at the rate at which you pay tax.

Where income from self-employment or even part-time employment differs from ordinary wage- or salary-earning status is that you are allowed, in assessing your earnings, to deduct from your profits any revenue expenditure 'wholly and exclusively incurred' in carrying on your trade or profession. Under the heading of revenue expenditure comes business expenses, and since your profits and your earnings will be either synonymous or closely related, the first point to observe is that you must claim all the business expenses to which the taxman entitles you.

Principal allowable business expenses

The cost of goods bought for resale and materials bought in manufacturing This does not include capital expenditure like cars or machinery, though certain minor items like small tools or typewriters may be allowed under this heading.

The running costs of the business or practice Under this concession come heating, lighting, rent, rates, telephone, postage, advertising, cleaning, repairs (but not improvements of a capital nature), insurance, the use of special clothing. If you are using your home as office you can claim up to two-thirds of the running costs of the premises as a business expense — provided you can convince the taxman that you are indeed using as high a proportion of your house as this exclusively for business purposes. In the past some people have been advised not to make this type of claim at all, because of the probability that, on selling, they might have to pay Capital Gains Tax on the 'business' part of the sale, thus outweighing any income tax advantage. This situation has been effectively altered in the 1978 Budget. (See section below on Capital Gains Tax.)

Carriage, packing and delivery costs

Wages and salaries Any sums paid to full-time or part-time employees. You cannot, however, count any salary you and your partners are taking from the business, but you can pay your wife a salary (provided she is actually doing a reasonably convincing amount of work for you). This is an advantage if her income from other sources is less than £945 a year, because that first slice of earnings is free of tax — one of the reliefs we mentioned earlier.

Entertaining Entertainment of overseas customers. The tax office may want to establish some correlation between the amount of export business you do and the sums you are claiming for entertainment in this connection. You are also allowed to claim for entertaining your own staff.

Travel Hotel and travel expenses on business trips and in connection with soliciting business. You are not, however, allowed the cost of travel between home and office, if you have a regular place of work.

In addition to these expenses you can claim for the running costs of your car (including petrol) in proportion to the extent to which you use it for business purposes.

Interest Interest on loans and overdrafts incurred wholly in connection with business. This does not include interest on any money you or your partners have lent to the business.

Hire and hire purchase Hiring and leasing charges and hire element in hire-purchase agreement (not the actual cost, because this is a capital expense).

Insurance Every kind of business insurance, including that taken out on behalf of employees, but excluding your own National Insurance contributions and premiums paid on your personal life insurance (though these premiums are subject to $16\frac{2}{3}$ per cent personal tax relief).

The VAT element in allowable business expenses (unless you are a taxable trader for VAT purposes) This would include, for instance, VAT on petrol for your car. The VAT on the purchase of a motor car is allowable in all cases, since this cannot be reclaimed in your VAT return.

Certain legal and other professional fees You are allowed to claim for things like audit fees or court actions in connection with business, but not for penalties for breaking the law (eg parking fines!).

Subscriptions to professional or trade bodies

Bad debts These are bad debts actually incurred, though provision is generally allowed against tax in the case of specific customers whom you can show are unlikely to meet their obligations — for instance if their account is overdue and they are failing to respond to reminders. A general provision for a percentage of unspecified bad debts is not allowable against tax, however sensible it may be to make such provision in your accounts.

Trade debts owing to you are counted as income even if they have not been paid at the end of the accounting period. Likewise, debts owed by you are counted as costs, even if you are not going to pay them until the next accounting period.

Gifts Business gifts costing up to £2 per recipient per year (but excluding food, drink and tobacco). All gifts to employees are allowable, but generous employers should remember that the employee may have to declare them on *his* tax return if their value is substantial.

Capital allowances

The business expenses listed above are all revenue expenditure items, incurred in the day-to-day running of your affairs. There are also capital expenditure outlays, like the acquisition of motor cars, large items of machinery and permanent fixtures and fittings. Although these cannot be deducted from your profits as normal business expenses, there are concessions available on them under another heading. You will remember that in Chapter 8 we dealt with the subject of depreciation as an element to be allowed for in costing. The taxman employs a somewhat similar concept in considering the cost to the business of acquiring capital equipment.

1. The depreciation on a motor car can be deducted from your profits at the rate of 25 per cent a year as a 'writing down allowance'. However, in the case of cars costing more than £4000 this is limited to £1000 a year.
2. A writing down allowance is also given for other capital equipment (but not buildings). You can, in fact, take a

'first year allowance' which enables you to write off 100 per cent in the tax year of acquisition. It may, of course, not pay you to do it this way if you do not have profits to set it off against. In that case you can claim your allowance at the rate of 25 per cent a year. Each year, of course, the 25 per cent is claimed on the proportion that has not yet been written off. Thus, if you buy an offset machine for £500, in year one you claim 500 x (25/100) = £125; and in year two £375 x (25/100) = £94, and so on.

3. Equipment bought on hire purchase is eligible for the writing down allowance in respect of the capital element. The hire charges themselves can be claimed as business expenses, spread over the period of the agreement.

In calculating your writing down allowances you will have to take into account whether or not you are a taxable trader for VAT purposes (see page 114). If you are, you will already have reclaimed the VAT on your purchase in your quarterly or monthly VAT return. Thus capital allowances will be calculated on the net amount excluding VAT (except in the case of motor cars).

Stock valuation

If you are in a business which involves holding stock — which may be either finished goods for resale, work in progress or materials for manufacture — it must be valued at each accounting date. The difference in value between opening stock and closing stock represents the cost of sales. Obviously, therefore, if you value your closing stock on a different basis from the opening stock, this will affect the profit you show. If you value the same kind of items more highly it will depress the cost of sales and increase the apparent profit. If you value them on a lower basis the cost of sales will be increased and the profit decreased.

Example A			Example B		
Sales		£150	Sales		£150
Opening Stock 100 Rose bushes @ £1.00:	£100		*Opening Stock* 100 Rose bushes @ £1.00:	£100	
Closing Stock 50 Rose bushes @ £1.50:	£75		*Closing Stock* 50 Rose bushes @ 60p:	£30	
Cost of Sales		£25	Cost of Sales		£70
Profit		£125	Profit		£80

Plainly, then, it does not make sense for you to upvalue your closing stock in order to show a paper profit. Equally, you are not allowed to depress it artificially in order to achieve the reverse effect. However, if you can make a genuine case that some stock will have to be sold at a lower margin than the one you normally work to in order to be able to sell it within a reasonable time, then a valuation in the light of this fact will generally be accepted by the taxman.

Computing taxable profit

Normally your accountant will prepare a set of accounts for you for each year you are in business. Your accounting dates need not coincide with the tax year (ending 5th April). The profits shown in these accounts will be the basis of your assessment — a point we shall return to in the next section.

As we stated earlier, certain costs which are genuine enough from the point of view of your profit and loss account are nevertheless not allowable for tax purposes — eg entertaining of customers other than foreign buyers or their agents. You are also not allowed to charge depreciation against your profit (though remember you will receive a writing down allowance which, in the end, has a similar effect). These and other non-allowable expenses, therefore, must be added back to the profits.

Equally certain profits which you have made are to be deducted for the purposes of Schedule D assessment because they are taxed on a different basis and are subject to a return under another heading. Examples are gains from the disposal of capital assets, income from sub-letting part of your premises or interest paid by the bank on money being held in a deposit account.

Losses

If your business or professional occupation has made a loss on its accounting year — remember that from the tax point of view non-allowable expenses are added back to profits, and you will have to do the same in your return — you can have the loss set off against your other income for the tax year in which the loss was incurred and for the subsequent year. The set-off has to be made first of all against earned income and then, if you are still 'in credit', against unearned income. This is laid down because unearned income (ie income from investments) may be subject to a higher tax rate than the earned variety. However, you cannot set off business losses against liability for capital gains tax.

If your income for the year in which you made the loss and that of the subsequent year still does not exceed that loss, you can set off the balance against future profits; or you can carry the loss back and set it against earlier profits.

An important concession has been made in the 1978 Budget to sole traders and partnerships. From 1978 losses incurred in the first four years of a business can now be carried back against income from other sources — including salary — in the three years before commencing business as a self-employed person or partner.

The basis of assessment

Schedule D tax for an established business is normally assessed on the profits for the preceding tax year. Thus your tax assessment for the tax year ending 5th April 1978 — and which you have to pay in 1978 — will relate to the accounting year which ended in the tax year finishing 5th April 1977. Your *accounting* year, as we have just said, need not coincide with the taxman's year: 5th April to 5th April. You can, if you like, run it to the anniversary of your commencing business, or on a calendar year. However, in the first year of operations, you will be assessed either on the proportion of profits for the accounting year represented by the time from your starting date to the 5th April, or the actual profits during those months.

Thus, if you commenced business on the 1st October 1977

and your profit for the year ending 30th September 1978 is £1000, you will be taxed on the basis of six months' profit (1st October 1977 — 5th April 1978). This assessment will have to be met in 1978. It is not on a preceding year basis.

In the second tax year — in this instance, the one ending 5th April 1979 — your Schedule D tax will be based on the actual profit for the first 12 months of business: here, £1000.

In the third tax year you will be assessed on your declaration for the preceding year which, as we have seen, is still the profit in your first 12 months of operations: in this case again £1000. Thereafter you will be paying tax on the normal basis of the preceding year's profits.

The object of these somewhat tortuous manoeuvres is to put you into phase for paying tax on the latter basis; but it has the disadvantage that if your profits are high in the first twelve months and thereafter shade off, you will be paying more tax than you should be in the second and third year. You can, therefore, elect to be taxed on your actual profits for those years. You should take your accountant's advice on the best course of action. He may also be able to demonstrate technical advantages, in terms of taxation, in starting business just after, rather than just before the 5th April in calculating the basis of assessment over the opening three-year period of a business.

Spare-time work

Even though you have a full-time job which is being taxed under Schedule E and thus being taken care of under your employer's PAYE scheme, you may also have earnings from part-time employment in the evenings and weekends which you have to declare. Your employer need not know about this second income because you can establish with your tax inspector that the tax code which fixes the amount of PAYE you pay (see page 113) only relates to the income you receive from your employer.

Your spare-time income is also eligible for the allowances on expenses 'wholly and exclusively incurred' for business purposes. This means that it is most important that you should keep a proper record of incomings and outgoings. If your spare-time activities are on a small scale, you will not need to keep the kind of detailed books of account described in Chapter 4; but you should certainly maintain a simple cash book, from which at the end of the year you or your accountant can prepare a statement to append to your income-tax return.

Tax on spare-time work is payable in two half-yearly assessments: on the 1st January within the year of assessment and on the 1st July following the end of it.

Probably the largest item you will be able to set off against spare-time income is any sums you can pay your wife for her assistance up to the level of her tax-free allowance of £625 and provided she is not earning as much as this from another source.

Partnerships

Partnership income is assessed between the partners in the same ratio as that in which they have agreed to split profits. However, the ratio will be the one that actually exists at the time the assessment is made which, since the tax is on a preceding year basis, may not necessarily be the same as that which obtained the year the profits were established.

Salaries, and interest on money put into the business by partners, are considered as profits for tax purposes and have to be added back as such in order to arrive at taxable profits.

For the purposes of assessment, the partnership is treated as a single entity — ie the tax will be collected from the partnership as a whole, not from the individuals that constitute it.

Corporation tax

Corporation Tax is payable by limited companies. Its provisions are somewhat complicated and it must be assumed, for the purposes of this brief chapter on taxation, that readers who are intending to set up businesses in this form will seek professional advice on tax aspects. However, the salient points are as follows:

1. Corporation tax is charged at a rate of 52 per cent on profits, though for companies with profits under £50,000 the rate is 42 per cent.
2. Dividends are paid to shareholders without deduction of tax, but 34/66ths of the dividends must be handed over to the Revenue by the company within three months of the date of payment of the dividend. This is known as 'Advance Corporation Tax' and is set off

against the Corporation Tax payable on profits.

3. Unlike Schedule D Income Tax, Corporation Tax is normally payable nine months from the end of each accounting period.

4. Allowable expenses against profits for Corporation Tax purposes are roughly the same as those for other forms of revenue expenditure, with the important addition that salaries paid to employees (who include the owners of the company, if they are working in it) are deductible. However, in certain circumstances, the interest on loans made to the company by directors will not be treated as an allowable expense, but as a distribution of income on which Advance Corporation Tax is payable.

If you are a director of a limited company, your income from this source will not be liable to the National Insurance levy of five per cent on income between £2000 and £6250 a year. Your National Insurance contribution will be at the employed rate and you will be paying PAYE on your salary.

5. 'Close companies' which, broadly speaking, are the kind of small, family-owned companies which are likely to be formed by our readers may in effect be directed by the Revenue to distribute profits over and above the amount they have elected to do, if the amount of such potentially distributable profits exceeds £1001. However, exemption from such direction can be granted if the company is able to show that the money is needed in the business; for instance to finance expansion of trade.

Capital Transfer Tax and Capital Gains Tax

Capital Transfer Tax was introduced in 1974 to replace Estate Duty and was potentially disastrous for many small businesses which having no liquid assets with which to pay the tax, would ultimately have been faced with no alternative but to sell out — when their proprietors would have come up against the further hurdle of Capital Gains Tax.

A major new concession has been introduced in the 1978 Budget which without going into technicalities, means that ownership of a firm can be handed on to a second party — not necessarily a member of the family, apparently — without liability for CTT or CGT arising until the business is actually

112

sold to a third party. At the same time, people who have been owners of a business for more than 10 years can, at the age of 60, obtain relief from CGT if they do sell their assets — at the rate of £10,000 a year for every year by which they are over 60 and up to a maximum of £50,000. Previously the maximum figure was only £20,000.

Another significant new concession on CGT is concerned with the so-called 'rollover' relief on business assets. This means that if you sell a business asset at a profit but replace it with another one, that profit does not attract CGT.

This benefit is of particular interest to, among others, people who have been claiming tax relief on the business use of part of their private house. Up to 1978 they would have been in the position of having to pay CGT on the proportion of the house when they came to selling it, assuming a capital gain arose — as it generally would have done during a period of continuing inflation in house prices. This fact deterred a number of Schedule D taxpayers from claiming use of their house as a business expense. Now they can sell at will and, of course, if they retire and give up business they will fall within the scope of the retirement relief provisions, thus escaping this kind of CGT altogether.

Appeals

Every taxpayer, be he an individual or a corporation, has the right to appeal against his assessment, if he has grounds for believing he is being asked to pay too much. Such appeals have to be made in writing to the Inspector of Taxes within 30 days of receiving an assessment. They are usually settled by more or less amicable correspondence, but ultimately can be taken to a hearing by the General or Special Commissioners.

PAYE

If you employ staff you will be responsible for deducting PAYE from their wages. The same applies to your own salary from a partnership or a limited company. The sums have to be paid monthly to the Inland Revenue by the employer.

You will receive from the tax office a tax deduction card for each employee, with spaces for each week or month (depending on how they are paid) for the year ending 5th April. On these cards, weekly or monthly as the case may

113

be, you will have to enter under a number of headings, details of tax, pay for each period and for the year to date. You will know how much tax to deduct from reading off the employee's tax code number, which has been allotted to him by the tax office, against a set of tables with which you will also be issued. Without going too far into technicalities, the way the tables work is to provide a mechanism, self-correcting for possible fluctuations of earnings, of assessing the amount of tax due on any particular wage or salary at any given point of the year.

At the end of the tax year you will have to make out two forms:

1. Form P 60 issued to each employee. This gives details of pay and tax deducted during the year.
2. Form P 35 for the Inland Revenue. This is a summary of tax and graduated National Insurance contributions for all employees during the year.

When an employee leaves, you should complete another form, P 45, for him. Part of this form, showing his code number, pay and tax deducted for the year to date, is sent to the tax office. The other parts are to be handed by the employee to his new employer so that he can pick up the PAYE system where you left off.

VAT

If the taxable outputs of your business — which for practical purposes means what you charge your customers for any goods or services that are not specifically 'exempt' — exceed, or are likely to exceed £10,000 a year, you will have to register with the Customs and Excise (not the tax office, in this case) as a taxable trader for VAT purposes. This means that you will have to remit to Customs and Excise, either monthly or quarterly, eight per cent of the price you charge — your outputs', this being the current standard rate of VAT (except for petrol and some 'luxury' goods at 12½ per cent). However, you will be able to deduct from these remittances any VAT which you yourself have been charged by your suppliers — your 'inputs'. This item covers not only materials used in producing the goods or services you supply to your customers, but everything which you have to buy to run your business — including such things as telephone charges.

114

Not all goods and services carry VAT. Some are 'zero rated' — basic foodstuffs, newspapers and exported goods being notable examples. (Full details are contained in VAT Notices 700 and 701, issued by Customs and Excise, Kings Beam House, Mark Lane, London EC3, and you should obtain these from them, together with any other Notices about VAT which are relevant to your trade or profession.) The significance of zero rating is that even though you do not charge VAT on goods of this nature that you supply, you can still claim back VAT on all your inputs, excluding the purchase of cars and business entertainment of domestic customers.

Zero rating is not, however, the same as 'exemption'. Zero rating carries a theoretical rate of VAT, which is 0 per cent. Exemption means that no rate of VAT applies at all and examples of exempt suppliers are bookmakers, persons selling or renting land and buildings, and various types of medical services. The exempt status is not particularly desirable, because if you are exempt you still have to pay VAT on all your inputs but have no outputs to set the tax off against.

In this sense exempt traders are like private individuals and the question, therefore, arises as to whether you should, as you are entitled to do, ask to be registered as a taxable trader even though your outputs are less than the mandatory £10,000 a year level. (Customs and Excise may, of course, refuse to register you on the grounds that your outputs are too low, though no hard-and-fast minimum figure for this has been fixed.) Your accountant should be able to advise you on this point, but the main consideration would be the level of your taxable inputs. Thus if you are a part-time cabinetmaker you would be buying a lot of materials which carry VAT. But if you were doing something like picture research, the VAT inputs might be quite low and the administrative work involved in being a taxable trader might not be justified by the amount of VAT you could claim back against your outputs.

The point to be realised is that if you register as a taxable trader, voluntarily or otherwise, you are going to be involved in a fair bit of extra administration. At the end of each VAT accounting period (quarterly or monthly, the latter being more usual with traders in zero-rated goods) you are going to have to make a return of all your outputs, showing their total value and the amount of VAT charged. Against this you set the total of your inputs and the amount of VAT you have

115

paid. The difference between the VAT on your outputs and that on your inputs is the sum payable to Customs and Excise. This obviously causes problems for retailers making a great many small sales and particularly for those supplying a mixture of zero-rated and standard-rated goods (e g a shop supplying sweets, which are taxable and other items of foods which are mostly zero-rated). It also underlines the vital importance of keeping proper records and retaining copy invoices of all sales and purchases, because although your VAT return need only show totals, Customs and Excise inspectors are empowered to check the documents on which your return is based. There is obviously, therefore, a link between the records you have to maintain for ordinary accounting purposes and those that are needed to back up your VAT return.

There is also a close connection between VAT and the all-important business of cash flow. When you receive an invoice bearing VAT, the input element can be set off against the VAT output on your next return, irrespective of whether you yourself have paid the supplier. Therefore, if you are buying an expensive piece of capital equipment it will make sense for you to arrange to be invoiced just before your next return to Customs and Excise is due.

The boot is on the other foot, though, when you yourself are extending credit to a customer. The sale is reckoned to have taken place when the invoice has been rendered, not when you have received payment. Therefore you will be paying VAT on your output before you have actually received the cash covering it from your customer. This also means that except in some special cases no relief is given in respect of bad debts.

11:Employing People

A fairly common observation about employing people has always been to say that this is when your troubles begin. Today this is truer than ever, because apart from the difficulty of finding Mr or Ms Right — a task which even experienced personnel people admit, in their more candid moments, is something of a lottery — a mass of legislation has been enacted in recent years which, it is thought by some, favours the rights of employees at the expense of those of employers. Though the aim of this legislation has mainly been to protect the workforce of larger companies from arbitrary hiring and firing, it embraces even the smallest employer and to a large extent it covers part-time as well as full-time employees. Whole books could be and have been written about the legal technicalities involved, but all we can do in this section is to draw the reader's attention to some of the major pitfalls you should look out for when you start employing people.

The Contract of Employment

The contract of employment statement which has to be issued in writing to every employee who is going to work for you for 16 hours or more per week within four weeks of joining is in fact not a pitfall, but a rather sensible document which clarifies right from the outset what the terms of employment are. From the employer's point of view, the necessity of drafting a contract of employment statement should concentrate the mind wonderfully on issues about which it is all too easy to be sloppy at the expense of subsequent aggravation — such as hours of work, holidays and, above all, exactly what it is the employee is supposed to be doing. The following points have to be covered in the contract, and you must say so if you have not covered one or other of them:

The rate of pay and how it is calculated
Whether it is paid weekly or monthly
The normal hours of work and the terms and conditions relating to them
Holidays and holiday pay
Provision for sick pay
Pension and pension schemes
Notice required by both parties
The job title
Any disciplinary rules relating to the job
Grievance procedures

Unfair dismissal

Probably the area of legislation which it is easiest and most common to fall foul of is that relating to unfair dismissal. Every employee — and this includes part-timers if they work for you in other than a freelance capacity for more than 16 hours a week — who has been on your staff for 26 weeks or more must he given a written statement of your reasons if you want to dismiss him; you must also give him one week's notice (or payment in lieu) if he has been with you continuously for four weeks or more and, after two years, one week's notice for every year of continuous employment. Fair enough, you might say — particularly as, on the face of things, what the law regards as fair grounds for dismissal are perfectly reasonable: incompetence, misconduct or genuine redundancy. The problem is that the employee is at liberty to disagree with you on the fairness issue and to take his case to an industrial tribunal.

If he has been guilty of gross misconduct, such as persistently coming late to work, you will probably win your case, provided you warned him in writing to mend his ways well before you dismissed him. The point here is that you must not only have good reasons for dismissing him, but you must also have acted reasonably in the dismissal situation. This means that you have got to follow a proper sequence of written warnings — not less than three is the number generally recommended — stating his inadequacies, telling him what he has to do to put them right and spelling out the consequences if he fails to do so.

118

When it comes to matters of competence, though, things are rather less clear-cut, particularly if the task involved is not one where performance can be readily quantified or where there are a lot of imponderables. It would be relatively easy to argue a case against a machine operator who was consistently turning out less work than his colleagues on similar machines, but far more difficult in the case of a salesman who could plead that a poor call-rate was due to difficulties in finding car parking or inefficient back-up from the office.

The fact is that in all matters affecting competence you really have to do your homework very carefully before dismissing someone because some industrial tribunals at least have a reputation of giving the employee the benefit of any doubt that exists. Unfortunately, there often is doubt towards which the inexperienced employer may have unwittingly contributed by such steps as including the person concerned in a general salary rise not long before informing him he is not up to the job.

Likewise there can be cases where you, as the employer, may be satisfied in your mind that dismissal is fair, but where the law does not agree with you. One where you have to be very careful, for instance, is dismissal on medical grounds. Of course no reasonable employer would dismiss anyone in such circumstances if he could help it, but if you get stuck with someone who is persistently off sick and is able to provide satisfactory medical evidence you would have to show proof that the absences were of such a nature as to cause disruption to your business before you could discharge him. Even more tricky is the case of employees who are engaged in public duties, like being on the local council. You have to give them reasonable time off to attend those duties, though not necessarily with pay.

We have used the word 'he' of employees so far — in the interests of brevity, not for sexist reasons — but of course all these provisions extend to women as well. In face, quite apart from the Sex Discrimination Act and the Equal Pay Act — both of which mean, in essence, that women have in all respects to be treated on an equal footing with men — there are some additional hazards to employing women when they are of child-bearing age. Provided she works until 11 weeks before her confinement a woman who has been continuously in your employ for two years or more is entitled to take 40 weeks off if she becomes pregnant and to return to her original job, without loss of seniority, at the end of that time. Furthermore, she is entitled to full pay for the first six weeks of her absence, though the employer can recover the money from the Department of Employment. And if you bring in a replacement for her — or any other employee who is off for any longer period of time — be very careful as well. Even a temporary replacement could sue you for unlawful dismissal unless you notify him or her in writing that the appointment is a temporary one and give notice when it is coming to an end.

The penalties for losing an unfair dismissals case can be ruinous for a small firm. In the most extreme instances you could be in for a compensation award of £5200, plus any redundancy pay to which the employee is entitled, plus a basic award related to age and length of service of up to £2400. Thus if you are in any doubt at all about a dismissal situation you should consult a solicitor who is versed in this aspect of the law.

Redundancy

Redundancy, because it has become something of a euphemism for getting or giving the sack, is a ripe area for misunderstanding. In fact, although redundancy is a cause for dismissal it is not actually the same thing as dismissal, but occurs when a job disappears, eg because a firm ceases trading or has to cut down on staff. It is therefore not set about with the same kind of restrictions as dismissal, but nevertheless it does involve some financial penalties for employers if the employee has been continuously employed by the firm concerned for two years or more. In that case he will be entitled to redundancy pay on a formula based on length of service and rate of pay and up to a maximum of £2400. About half of this can in fact be recovered from the Department of Employment, whom you should notify if you intend to make anyone redundant. As usual, there is a good deal of form-filling involved. The law also requires you to give advance warning to the relevant unions if any of their members are to be made redundant.

What happens if you buy a business, lock, stock and barrel, together with the staff? You may find that you don't like some of the people the previous owner took on, or that you want to change or drop some of the things he was doing, with the result that staff will be made redundant. Irrespective of the fact that you did not hire the people concerned, you are still stuck with your responsibility towards them as their current employer, so that being the proverbial new broom can be a very costly exercise. Before buying a business, therefore, it is very important to look at the staff and at the extent of any redundancy payments or dismissals situations you could get involved in.

In the same context, another Act of Parliament you should keep an eye open for when buying a business is the Health and Safety at Work Act which lays down standards to which working premises have to conform. Before putting down your money you should check with the inspectors of the Health and Safety Executive that any premises you are buying or leasing as part of the deal meet those standards.

Recruitment

The cost of discharging staff, whether because of redundancy or by dismissal, makes it imperative that you should make the right decisions in picking people to work for you in the first place. We have said that the sphere of personnel selection is something of a lottery. It could equally be described as a gamble and there are ways in which you could cut down on the odds against you.

The most obvious question to ask yourself, of course, is whether you really do need to take someone on permanently at all. The principle we have put forward for the purchase of equipment — never buy anything outright unless you are sure you have a continuing use for it and that it will pay for itself over a reasonable interval of time — also applies to personnel. The legal constraints that cover part-time or full-time employees do not extend to freelances, personnel from agencies or outside work done on contract, and this could well be the best way of tackling a particular problem such as an upward bump in demand until you are sure that it is going to last. It is worth remembering, too, that when you take on staff you take on a good many payroll and administrative overheads in addition to their salary. These can add quite significantly to your costs.

Sooner or later, though, if you want your business to grow — and growth of some kind seems to be an inevitable concomitant of success — you are going to need people. But even then you should ask yourself what exactly you need them for and how much you can afford to pay. Clarifying these two issues is not only important for itself, but it will also give you the basis of a job description which you can use in your press advertising or approach to a recruitment agency, at the interview and, finally, in the contract of employment. Around it you should also build a series of questions to ask the interviewee that should give you some indication of his competence to do the job. Such questions should call for a detailed response rather than a 'yes' or 'no' type of answer; for instance, if you are interviewing a sales representative, asking him how long he has been in the business will tell you something, but not nearly as much as the answer to a question that tries to elicit which buyers he knows and how well he knows them.

Competence is part of the story. Equally important is the interviewee's track record — how many previous employers he has had and whether his progress has been up, down or steady. Too many job changes at frequent intervals can be a bad sign and it is fair to ask searching questions about this if it is part of the employment pattern. It is also wise to be cautious about people who are willing to take a large drop in salary. In these days when good jobs are hard to come by there can be a perfectly good reason for this, but you ought to tactfully find out what it is.

Possibly the references will give you a clue and you should always ask for and check references. They are not always reliable — most employers are kindly people and they will not speak ill of an ex-employee if they can help it — but they will generally alert you to real disaster areas. Telephone reference checks are widely reckoned to be more reliable than written ones because referees are nearly always more forthcoming in conversation than in a letter, since the law of libel and, nowadays, industrial relations law looms large in any written deposition.

Checklist: employing people

1. Do you really need to take on staff? Will there be enough to keep them busy a year from now?
2. Have you worked out a job description which sets out the purpose of the job, the duties involved and who the person appointed will report to?
3. Have you decided how much you can afford to pay?
4. Do your advertisements or approach to a recruiting agency spell out the job description, the salary and the approximate age of the person you are looking for?

5. Does it in any way contravene the Sex Discrimination Act or the Race Relations Act?
6. Have you prepared a series of questions that will throw some light on the interviewee's competence, personality and previous record of employment?
7. Have you taken up and checked references?
8. Are you satisfied, before making the appointment, that you have seen enough applicants to give you an idea of the quality of staff available for this particular job?
9. Do you have a procedure for reviewing the employee's progress before the expiry of the 26-week period after which he can claim unfair dismissal if you decide he is not suitable?

DECIDE
FOR YOURSELF

When you work for yourself, no-one else will make your decisions for you. You will need to consider how best to provide for your retirement and protect your family.

Perhaps you feel that you do not need a pension scheme or any arrangement to provide cash in the event of death or disability. After all, if the worst comes to the worst, you could always sell your business. However, the price you will get will depend on how the business is trading at the time. Wouldn't it be better to make provision in those years when business is at its best?

Pensions arrangements have always enjoyed favourable tax treatment. The right type of scheme can make a considerable difference to your tax bill.

Notcutt's can offer a wide range of schemes for people who work for themselves, for partnerships or for small limited companies. We also have a specialist department to advise on the particular problems of partnership schemes and Capital Transfer Tax.

For further information contact:

NOTCUTT LIFE AND PENSIONS LIMITED
Mackenzie House, 221 Beckenham Road, Beckenham Kent BR3 4UB
Telephone 01-778 7878

12:Pensions

by C B Cochran, *Pensions Consultant*

Although the government has made a number of concessions to the self-employed in recent budgets, one area where
they have been more or less left out in the cold is that of
state pensions. While the rest of the working population is
entitled to two pensions — the basic state pension plus an
earnings-related scheme — the self-employed qualify only
for the former. The problem is, of course, that it is very
difficult to base an earnings-related scheme on a figure which,
as happens in the case of the self-employed, may fluctuate
from year to year. This, however, is very little consolation to
anyone who, not having made any other provision, faces retirement on a state pension which, for married couples, only
amounts to £28 a week — £50 less than the national average
wage.

The implication of all this would appear to be that the
government have left the self-employed to shift for themselves as far as pensions are concerned, and they have in fact
made a number of tax concessions which will have the effect
of lightening the burden of making your own pension
arrangements. For one thing the National Insurance contribution has been lowered from £2.66 for a man and £1.90
for a women to £1.90 for either sex. Since the flat rate
benefit remains unchanged at £17.50 a week the contribution
reduction represents a real though small gain.

A more significant step is that in the 1978 Budget the
Class 4 National Insurance contribution from self-employed
net profits has been lowered from 8 per cent to 5 per cent and
the lower end of the profits band on which the levy is payable
has been raised from £1750 to £2000; on the other hand, the
upper band has been raised too — from £5500 to £6250.

More significant still are concessions introduced over a
number of Finance Acts, relating to earnings earmarked for

private pensions.

Firstly, full tax relief may be claimed on 15 per cent of net earnings (earnings after allowable expenses) if these are applied to a private pensions plan. The 15 per cent would, of course, be applied at the top rate of tax, making this a considerable benefit to high taxpayers. On the other hand, since the government seldom gives with one hand what it does not, at least in some measure, take away with the other, the maximum sum that can be claimed is £3000 (increased from £2250 in the 1978 Budget). This means that if you earn in excess of £15,000 you can claim tax relief on any amount up to £3000 which you are paying into a private pension scheme. Furthermore, if your contribution adds up to over 15 per cent of net earnings, the excess can be carried forward to future years, when you hope your income will be high enough to enable tax relief to be claimed. This obviously makes sense in view of the fluctuation which is apt to occur in self-employed income and which itself, as has been pointed out above, makes it difficult to integrate you in an earnings-related state scheme.

Also, your contributions can be backdated for tax purposes within six months of your assessment for the year. Thus, if your accounts for the year to 31st December 1978 are not agreed by your accountant and the Inspector of Taxes until the 30th September 1979, you will have until 30th March 1980 to pay and lodge with the Inland Revenue a claim to have your pension contribution allowed against your profits for the year to December 1978.

Apart from the personal tax relief element, there are three other reasons why making provision for a private pension plan provides some kind of haven aganist the tax blizzard.

Firstly, all contributions are invested in a special pensions fund which does not pay tax, hence the rate of growth is significantly greater than an ordinary savings fund. Secondly, a tax free cash sum is payable when you begin your pension; and thirdly, the pension itself is taxed as earned and not as investment income. So the advantages of personal pensions are considerable, even for those people who are only able to claim relief at a lower rate.

These advantages can be extended if you are paying your wife a salary as your employee. You will remember from the tax chapter that the Inland Revenue currently allows £985 to be paid tax free to your wife in these circumstances. They will also allow her to have a pension of two-thirds of her final

Pension problem?

Personal pensions

A CRUSADER SCHEME FOR THE
SELF-EMPLOYED, CONTROLLING DIRECTORS,
EMPLOYEES WITH NO PENSION RIGHTS

EXAMPLE FOR MAN AGED 45 NEXT BIRTHDAY
Invests £500 per annum to retire at 65
Net annual cost £330 (Tax Relief at 34%)
Net total cost £6,930
Possible Pension
£5,907p.a. FOR LIFE
or £13,096 cash and £3,981 p.a. for life

EXAMPLE FOR WOMAN AGED 40 NEXT BIRTHDAY
Invests £500 per annum to retire at 60
Net annual cost £330 (Tax Relief at 34%)
Net total cost £6,930
Possible pension
£4,901p.a. FOR LIFE
or £11,117 cash and £3,494 p.a. for life

EXAMPLE FOR MAN AGED 50 NEXT BIRTHDAY
Invests £750 per annum to retire at 65
Net annual cost £495.00 (Tax Relief at 34%)
Net total cost £7,920
Possible pension
£4,695p.a. FOR LIFE
or £10,409 cash and £3,164 p.a. for life

EXAMPLE FOR WOMAN AGED 45 NEXT BIRTHDAY
Invests £400 per annum to retire at 60
Net annual cost £264 (Tax Relief at 34%)
Net total cost £4,224
Possible Pension
£2,080p.a. FOR LIFE
or £4,718 cash and £1,483 p.a. for life

This leaflet is worth reading.

If you are self-employed, a controlling director, or an employee with no pension rights, it could give you the answer on how to provide a substantial retirement income with a degree of flexibility geared to your precise requirements.

earnings and one which will increase upwards at 8½ per cent per annum. Thus for a woman of 35 it is possible to invest up to £1000 per annum in a pension scheme to provide a pension at 60. This £1000 will count as a normal business expense by her husband in the same way as the salary itself and would be allowed against his highest rate of tax on earned income.

This would be more profitable than spending the same amount on the husband's pension, as that would probably increase his tax liability after retirement.

Leaving aside this option, however, we show in the table below four possible methods for someone aged 40 to save £500 per annum towards a retirement pension on their 65th birthday. This illustrates the benefit on the tax position of investing in a pension fund, as compared to other forms of savings.

While there are many types of plan available, basically they fall into three main categories: deferred annuity, cash-funded, and unit-linked.

Deferred annuities give a policyholder a basic guaranteed pension. In addition, each year a further bonus pension attachment based on a share of the pension fund profits may be added. These then become guaranteed in the same way as bonus attachments to with-profit endowment policies. Companies offering this type of contract include the Legal and General, the National Provident Institution and the Sun Alliance.

The cash-funded method is rather similar to saving in a building society account. Regular contributions are made and each year bonuses are added to the contributions to increase the size of the account. A large pool of money, therefore, accumulates and at retirement this pool is used to buy a pension at the then going rate. As this can and does fluctuate, companies offer a guaranteed basic pension, but this is usually 20-30 per cent below the likely current market rate. Companies offering this kind of scheme include the Norwich Union, the Standard Life, and the United Kingdom Provident Institution.

Unit-linked contracts are probably best considered by those people who already have a secured and reasonably guaranteed income on retirement. Each year the contribution made is deemed to buy units at the current price. At retirement all these units are cashed in and the money is used to buy a pension at the current going rate. This is a very

	Under The Bed	Building Society Savings Account	Endowment With Profits	Personal Pension Tax Paid 33%
Total Contribution	£12,500.00	£12,500.00	£12,500.00	£12,500.00
* Interest on Share Account/ + Bonus on Endowment/ † Accumulation of Pension Fund	Nil	£14,786.00*	£20,669.00+	£35,642.00†
Total Investment	£12,500.00	£27,286.00	£33,169.00	£48,142.00
Annual Pension	£1,669.00	£3,710.00	£4,511.00	£4,650.00
Tax Free Cash Sum				£13,951.00
Net Cost	£12,500.00	£12,500.00	£10,437.00	£8,375.00

Table I   *The three types of pension plan*

similar arrangements in method to the cash-funded plans, though because of the fluctuation in the stock market a less secure way of saving for a pension. Leading unit-linked offices offering this type of plan are the Abbey Life, Hambro Life and the M & G. The amount of unit-linked pension depends very much on how the value of the units have grown over the period. Similarly, bonuses and interest make up a considerable part of the deferred annuity and the cash-funded pensions, so it follows that whatever contract is chosen it is best to chose a company which already has a good investment record.

A self-employed person is allowed to take his pension between the ages of 60 to 75, even lower for some special categories. However, many of the self-employed may wish to work part-time before they retire, and therefore to take a portion of their pension at the outset just to top up their earnings, and then to take the remainder when they finally retire. If this is the case it would be worthwhile looking to those companies which offer flexible pension arrangements. These include the Legal and General, and the Scottish Amicable.

Finally, as with any other investment, you need to take advice and this comes best either from a pensions consultant with one of the larger firms of insurance brokers or alternatively direct from an insurance company.

M&G's NEW PENSION OFFER

The M&G Personal Pension Plan now provides a choice between guaranteed and unit-linked. There is complete tax exemption and no commitment to regular premiums. Anyone who is self-employed or not a member of a company scheme can join.

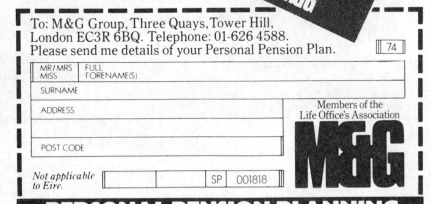

Part 2: Opportunities

Introduction

Self-employment falls into three main categories:

1. Running a business, such as a shop, pub or hotel, keeping a farm or market garden or taking up a franchise.
2. Providing a service, such as window-cleaning, painting and decorating, catering, hairdressing etc.
3. Freelance marketing of your skills or talents, eg cabinet-making, upholstery, making jewellery or pottery, writing for newspapers or magazines, photography, selling produce or crafts from a stall, translating etc.

There are obviously hundreds of examples within each category. The self-employed range from window-cleaners to tax consultants, from the couple running a corner sweet shop to the famous author living in his tax haven abroad. In this section of the book we cover some of the more popular areas within each category. If the area you are particularly interested in is not covered here, the best advice we can give is to talk to someone who has tried it (and preferably someone who has been successful).

1: Running a Business

Back to the land

The 'back to the land' movement has been quite fashionable in recent years, with all kinds of people giving up their jobs and homes in cities to live on smallholdings (communal or otherwise) where they try to be completely self-sufficient. Others, more commercially minded, may take up market gardening, which gives them a pleasant life in the country while they sell the fruits of their labours to others. Some more conventional souls may simply decide to buy a farm and rear cattle, grow corn or even keep pigs.

In all cases, the romantic glow soon disappears. There are two essentials for any of these occupations, neither of them romantic: lots of capital and the capacity for hard work. Take all the advice you can, from professional bodies such as the Ministry of Agriculture's Advisory Service or the local county office of the National Farmer's Union. The local authority is responsible for agricultural education and you should make enquiries about courses that might be available in your area. The soaring costs of fuel and animal feedstuffs have already put many market gardeners and farmers out of business, so it's obviously essential to go into the finances of the operation very thoroughly before making a decision.

Note: Addresses of bodies mentioned in the text are given on pages 219 to 227. Details of publications are given in the bibliography, pages 228 to 229.

It's also essential to have the complete support of your family. This can be a very hard life, getting up early in all weathers to feed animals, breaking your back hoeing and weeding, and you have to be extremely keen and enthusiastic to take it on. If your nearest and dearest is not equally enthusiastic — forget it, for you are going to need their active help, since labour is both expensive and hard to come by.

Farming

The old joke that there are only three ways to get into farming — matrimony, patrimony and parsimony — applies even more strongly today. Unless you stand to inherit a farm, you are going to need an awful lot of money: agricultural land at the moment averages over £1000 an acre and good quality land regularly sells at £1700 plus an acre. The acreage you require will depend on the type of farming and the quality of the land — it could vary from 100 acres for dairy famring to, say, 300 acres for arable farming. And it doesn't stop there — you are then going to need working capital to buy cows, sheep, tractors, combines, etc. Even to start in a modest way could need £20,000 to £30,000 working capital.

You may be lucky enough to possess that kind of money, or at least have access to it; if not, you are going to need a bank loan, and here you are going to discover the other essential qualification for a farmer nowadays — technical know-how. Farming has become a technological occupation, requiring all kinds of special skills and knowledge. Unless you can convince a bank that you have this know-how (and some business experience) you are unlikely to get your money. Long-term loans for the purchase of land are available from the Agricultural Mortgage Corporation Ltd, but here again, properly-prepared budgets will be required if the application is to be successful.

Farming is now a highly risky occupation giving only a 3 to 4 per cent return on the land. The failure rate is very high, particularly among the kind of people who take it up, with absolutely no experience, because it seems to offer a pleasant way of life. Unless you know about fertilisers, pesticides, animal husbandry, farm machinery, you are likely to make some expensive mistakes — and remember that two bad years could wipe you out financially. The

137

farmers who are most successful are those who start young, probably in a family-owned business. By the time they take over, they have acquired the necessary experience — usually backed up these days with a course at one of the agricultural colleges. You should not really even contemplate farming without some practical experience, or a degree or diploma from one of the agricultural colleges — see *British Quali-fications* for details of courses.

A cheaper way in is to try to become a tenant farmer — you don't have the enormous expense of buying the land, but once in you are protected for life and can run things to suit yourself (except for mismanagement of course). The snag is that tenancies are in tremendous demand — there are often as many as 100 applicants for one farm. You can also try intensive farming, where you again save on the cost of land, though remember that here your working capital require-ments are going to be higher — battery hens or other animals require a lot of outlay in the form of equipment and feedstuffs, while market gardeners will find themselves spending a fortune on heating greenhouses. Soaring costs in fact have meant that intensive farming is not so profitable as it was, and a lot of people have gone out of business. The trend in farming at the moment is in fact towards bigger, not smaller, units, because it is the only way to make a decent living.

Another idea which is very popular at the moment with the 'get-away-from-it-all-brigade' is to buy a smallholding and try to be entirely self-sufficient, perhaps even setting up a commune. It's an attractive idea, and the initial cost need not be great, but be warned — this is subsistence farming and you'll find yourself working as hard as the American pioneers did. Also, even on a commune you might need a tractor, say, to lift potatoes, etc and for that, you are going to need money. You really need to be dedicated, or rich (prefer-ably both).

If the foregoing has not deterred you, get some profes-sional advice, either from ADAS (The Agricultural Develop-ment Advisory Service of the Ministry of Agriculture) or from your local agricultural college or institute. There are also various farm-management consultants and land agency firms who will (for a fee) give advice on what to do.

Market gardening

Unless you take over an established business, the main problems for the would-be market gardener are acquiring the necessary land and a greenhouse. You may be lucky enough to already own a suitable piece of land, or a garden big enough (two to three acres) to be worked commercially, otherwise you may have to pay anything up to £2000 an acre. A greenhouse is the other big expense. It's a pretty vital piece of equipment, enabling you to grow tomatoes, bedding plants, pot plants for the winter months and seedlings for early vegetables. You can do without one, but you must then make enough money in the spring and summer to make up for the lean winter months when you have virtually nothing to offer except a few winter vegetables. You also have to make provision for the cost of heating a greenhouse: recent price increases in fuel have sent the cost sky-high, so you must make sure that every inch of space is working for you, if your profits are not going literally to disappear in smoke. Even the cheapest second-hand greenhouse is likely to cost at least £1000, while a new one costs five to six times as much.

If you are not a trained horticulturalist yourself, it's a good idea to employ someone who is, or who has at least had practical experience of running a big garden and greenhouse. One full-time helper is probably all you will be able to afford in the early years. Seasonal help picking tomatoes, strawberries, beans, etc costs between 60p and 80p an hour, and is often difficult to find. You (and your family) must be prepared to work long hours and turn your hand to anything.

For general information, particularly on the economics of growing produce, contact the National Farmers' Union who have a very good horticultural section. Another excellent source of information on what crops to grow, soil tests, etc is the Agricultural Development Advisory Service of the Ministry of Agriculture.

One basic decision to be made, once you have decided on your crops, is how you are going to market your produce. If you are on a busy main road you may decide to rely heavily on local advertising and passing trade from tourists, etc, sending the surplus to the local market, or even taking a stall in the local market yourself. You can also send your produce to one of the big central markets, but you then have to pay a fee to the auctioneer, as well as transport costs.

Franchising

Martin Mendelsohn, author of *The Guide to Franchising* (Pergamon Press)

One method by which it is possible to start in business and reduce the risks inherent in such a venture is to take up a business format franchise.

The business format franchise is a stage in the development of agency, distributorship, licences, and know-how type of manufacturing and marketing transactions. Instead of being limited to one aspect of business activity there has developed the concept of licensing an entire package comprising all the elements necessary to establish a previously untrained person in a business to be run on a pre-determined basis. These elements comprise:

(a)   the entire business concept;
(b)   a process of initiation and training in all aspects of the running of the business acording to that concept; and
(c)   a continuing process of assistance and guidance.

(a)   The entire business concept

This involves the development by the franchisor of a successful way of carrying on a business in all its aspects. The franchisor will develop what may be described as a 'blueprint' for conducting the business. The blueprint should

(i)   eliminate so far as possible the risks inherent in open-a new business, eg, the product range should be thoroughly market tested in pilot operations run by the franchisor;
(ii)   enable a person who has never before owned or operated a business to open up in business on his own account, not only with a pre-established format but with the backing of an organisation (ie the franchisor) that would not otherwise be available to him;
(iii) set out in detail exactly how the business should be run.

(b)   Process of initation and training

The franchisee must be trained in the business methods that are necessary to operate the business according to the blueprint. This may involve training in the use of specialised

141

equipment, marketing methods, preparation of produce and application of processes. The franchisee should be trained so that he is relatively expert in those spheres that are necessary for the operation of that particular business.

(c) Continuing process of assistance and guidance

The franchisor will in many cases provide the following range of services on a continuing basis depending of course upon the particular type of business:

(i)   regular visits from and access to a 'trouble-shooter' to assist in correcting or preventing deviations from the blueprint which may cause trading difficulties for the franchisee;

(ii)   liaison between the franchisor, the franchisee and all other franchisees for exchanges of ideas and experiences;

(iii)   product or concept innovation including investigation of marketability and compatibility with the existing business;

(iv)   retraining facilities and training facilities, for the franchisee's staff;

(v)   market research;

(vi)   national and local advertising and promotion;

(vii)   bulk purchasing opportunities;

(viii)   management and accounting advice and services;

(ix)   publication of a journal;

(x)   research into methods.

It will be seen that the business format franchise is a comprehensive and continuing relationship in which the initial concept is always being developed. The resources available for such development are those contributed to by the franchisor and all franchisees and are therefore much more considerable than any one individual could reasonably afford.

It will be noted that reference has been made to the *business format franchise*. The expression *franchise* is now popularly used to describe all those transactions in which one person licenses another rights to do something. For example, petrol filling stations, car dealerships, the use of a sportsman's or entertainer's name are commonly called franchises. It is important that you recognise what sort of franchise you are dealing with so that it is clear what can really be expected.

The word franchising can be used as a vehicle for abuse

and indeed it already has been. It is the sort of transaction that readily lends itself to fraudulent practices. Invariably the transaction falls into two stages, the first is the provision of pre-opening services, the second the continuing relationship thereafter. If therefore the franchisor charges too much at stage one and is not there to provide stage two the fraud is obvious. A fraud could be committed by franchising an untried and undeveloped concept resulting in a franchisee being charged fees for a right to conduct a business which in reality does not exist.

Pyramid Selling

The most serious frauds which have been perpetrated upon the unsuspecting were described as pyramid selling or multi-level marketing schemes. These schemes are presented as fool-proof and very tempting methods of making easy money and are often marketed by presenting successful 'franchisees' who speak of their great financial success. These schemes involve the sale of distributorships to purchasers who may divide and sub-divide them and sell them on to those whom they recruit as sub-distributors. Expansion of these enterprises takes place on the chain letter principle.

The ostensible object is to build up a sales force which will sell the company's products or services from door to door. In fact, selling the goods or services is difficult; they are usually expensive and areas are often saturated with other distributors. Selling distributorships is much more lucrative and becomes effectively the company's business.

These schemes were quickly recognised by the government as containing elements which are dishonest and, accordingly, the Fair Trading Act 1973 contains provisions which prohibit pyramid-type schemes. The Act also contains provisions which permit the making of regulations

(a) to control or prohibit the issue, circulation or distribution of documents which contain invitations to persons to participate in a scheme; and

(b) prohibiting the promoter of a scheme from performing functions which are vital to the operation of such a scheme, eg supplying goods or receiving payment for goods.

It is important to be able to recognise involvement with a pyramid-type scheme. And obviously, before signing any con-

100 OF T
REASONS
CHOOSIN
ZIEBART

There are many rustproofing companies and all of them claim to be best. But there is one thing that separates Ziebart from the rest–their dealer network.
It is a fact that Ziebart have over 100 AA approved stations and it is that, together with their knowledge and expertise that make Ziebart *market leaders in the rustproofing field.

You can see on the map, the areas where Ziebart dealers are located. Further dealers are wanted in areas not indicated wit a shield, so, if you want to apply your drive and ambition to be with the market leaders and enjoy the high profit margins of the best vehicle rustproofing then contact:

Lou Smith, Ziebart GB Ltd,
Dominion Way, Worthing, Sussex.
Telephone Worthing 204171.

The Ziebart Network is growing fast, so
don't think about it too long – ACT NOW.

IE BEST
FOR
G

SEAL OF AA APPROVAL — THE AUTOMOBILE ASSOCIATION

Map showing Dealer Network in Britain

Ziebart
VEHICLE RUSTPROOFING

*TNA Survey 1977.

tract or parting with money you should take proper professional advice. Be suspicious if you are offered or told that there will be a reward (ie payment, supply of cheaper products or any other disguised benefit) for doing something totally unrelated to the sale of the basic product or service with which the scheme is involved. For example, you may be offered a percentage payment of any sum paid to the promoter of the scheme for recruiting another participant, or for persuading such participant to purchase a higher position in the scheme. Other rewards could include a profit or commission on sales, or the provision of services or training to other participants in the scheme, or a commission on sales effected by other participants in the scheme.

Advantages and disadvantages of franchising

Advantages to the franchisee

1. The franchisee's lack of basic or specialised knowledge is overcome by the training programme of the franchisor.
2. The franchisee has the incentive of owning his own business despite the background of assistance from the franchisor. He is an independent businessman within the framework of the franchise agreement and can by his own hard work and effort maximise the value of his investment.
3. The franchisee's business opens with the benefit of a name already well established in the mind and eye of the public.
4. The franchisee invariably requires less capital than is required in setting up independently by reason of the assistance given by the franchisor.

However, many franchised businesses are organised in a highly sophisticated way and a franchisee may well have a larger investment to make than he would if he were to open for business without the franchise umbrella. On the other hand a more modest investment may jeopardise the success of the business.

5. The franchisee should (where appropriate) receive assistance in
   (a) site selection;
   (b) preparation of plans for remodelling the premises,

146

including the obtaining of any necessary town planning or by-law consents;

(c) obtaining finance for the acquisition of the franchised business;

(d) the training of his staff;

(e) purchase of equipment;

(f) selection and purchase of stock;

(g) getting the business open and running smoothly.

6.   The francisee receives the benefit on a national scale (if appropriate) of the franchisor's advertising and promotional activities.

7.   The franchisee receives the benefit of the bulk purchasing and negotiating capacity of the franchisor on behalf of all the franchisees.

8.   The franchisee has at his fingertips the specialised and highly skilled knowledge and experience of the franchisor's Head Office organisation in all aspects of his business while continuing in a self-employed capacity.

9.   The franchisee's business risk is reduced. However, no franchisee should consider that because he is coming

under the umbrella of the franchisor he is not going to be exposed to any risk at all. Any business undertaking involves risk and a franchised business is no exception. To be successful, the franchisee will have to work hard, harder than ever before perhaps. The franchisor will never be able to promise great rewards for little effort. The blueprint for carrying on business successfully and profitably can rarely be the blueprint for carrying on business successfully without working.

10. The franchisee has the services of 'trouble-shooters' provided by the franchisor to assist him with the many problems that may arise from time to time in the course of business.

11. The franchisee has the benefit of the use of the franchisor's patents, trade marks, trade secrets and any secret process or formulae.

12. The franchisee has the benefit of the franchisor's continuous research and development programmes designed to improve the business and keep it up to date.

13. The franchisor obtains the maximum amount of market information and experience which is circularised for the benefit of all the franchisees. This should give him access to information which would not otherwise be available to him.

14. There are also usually some territorial guarantees to ensure that no competitive franchisee is set up in a competing business within a defined area around the franchisee's business address.

Disadvantages to the franchisee

1. Inevitably the relationship between the franchisor and franchisee will involve the imposition of controls. These controls will regulate the quality of the service or goods to be provided or sold by the franchisee. It has been mentioned previously that the franchisee will own his own business. He will, but he must accept that for the advantages enjoyed by him, by virtue of his association with the franchisor and all the other franchisees, control of quality and standards is essential. Each bad franchisee has an adverse effect not only on his own business, but indirectly on the whole franchised chain of business and all other franchisees. The franchisor will therefore

149

Want to run your own business?

✱ A still from the 1978/79 National Television Campaign.

Few opportunities can compare with becoming a Wimpy International Franchisee.

To begin with, we give you a head start in the shape of our world famous trademark. From the moment you open your doors everyone knows that you stand for good quality and good value. And you can't hope for two bigger money spinners than those.

But we help you long before you sell your first Wimpy hamburger. We help you choose your premises. We help you design them. We train you, and your staff and provide on-going operational support. We even help you keep the seats full with massive advertising support and major promotions.

And the capital commitment? Depending on the premises, £25,000 is an indication as to the likely sum required. Much of this can normally be financed and we'd be only too happy to advise on these matters.

If you'd like more information write to or call Mike Chambers at Wimpy International Ltd, 214 Chiswick High Road, London W4 1PH. Telephone: 01-994 6454.

WIMPY®

The Home of the Hamburger

demand that standards are maintained so that the maximum benefit is derived by the franchisee and indirectly by the whole franchised chain from the operation of the franchisee's business. This is not to say that the franchisee will not be able to make any contribution or to impose his own personality in his business. Most franchisors do encourage their franchisees to make their contribution to the development of the business of the franchise chain and hold seminars and get-togethers to assist in the process.

2. The franchisee will have to pay the franchisor for the services provided and for the use of the blueprint, ie franchise fees.

3. The difficulty of assessing the quality of the franchisor. This factor must be weighed very carefully by the franchisee for it can affect the franchisee in two ways. Firstly, the franchisor's offer of a package may well not amount to what it appears to be on the surface. Secondly, the franchisor may be unable to maintain the continuing services which the franchisee may need in order to sustain his efforts.

4. The franchise contract will contain some restrictions against the assignment of the franchised business. This is a clear inhibition on the franchisee's ability to deal with his own business but, as with most of the restrictions, there is a reason for it. The reason is that the franchisor will have already been most meticulous in his choice of the franchisee as his original franchisee for the particular outlet. Why then should he be any less meticulous in his approval of a replacement? Naturally he will wish to be satisfied that any successor of the franchisee is equally suitable for that purpose. In practice there is normally very little difficulty in the achievement of successful assignments of franchised businesses.

5. The franchisee may find himself becoming too dependent upon the franchisor. This can affect him in a number of ways; for example, he may not achieve the motivation that is necessary for him to work and build his business to take full advantage of the foundations that the blueprint provides.

6. The franchisor's policies may affect the franchisee's profitability.

7. The franchisor may make mistakes of policy; he may

151

make decisions relating to innovations in the business which are unsuccessful and operate to the detriment of the franchisee.

8. The good name of the franchised business or its brand image may become less reputable for reasons beyond the franchisee's control.

These, then, are the advantages and disadvantages which every franchisee must weight up and consider before making the decision on whether or not he wishes to enter into a franchised business. He must decide whether the advantages, with the training and support that they provide, are worth having in return for the surrender of independence to the degree of outside control which a franchise transaction entails. He must decide whether his franchisor is the right person with whom to do business; he must decide whether he is personally and temperamentally suitable for the type of relationship that a franchise involves.

Having weighed up all the factors and taken proper professional advice, the final decision rests with the franchisee. If he is not able to take this decision with confidence by himself after having heard all that his advisors have to say, he should consider whether he is the sort of person who is capable of running his own business.

There is not much guidance available in relation to franchising and it is recommended that you should make contact with the British Franchise Association and you should certainly obtain the free pamphlet on the subject published by The Small Firms Information Centre under the title *Obtaining a Franchise — A Guide for Small Firms*. There are those who describe themselves as franchise consultants but many of these represent franchisors and are trying to sell franchises. They may be more interested in selling you a franchise than giving you objective advice. Certainly discuss what you are proposing to do with your solicitor, your accountant, your bank manager or wife (or husband) and, if there is one, the trade organisation. One final word of caution. Any franchise proposition that is put to you that promises rich rewards for little work must be viewed with the greatest suspicion.

The hotel business

Before you even think of taking on a hotel, you must be quite sure that your family are behind you: running a hotel involves very long hours and a lot of hard work. If you are not going to get any cooperation (and active help) from the family, you would be well advised to forget the whole idea. This applies particularly if you have young children — who is going to look after them? Can you afford an au pair girl so that your wife is free to help run the business?

Once that problem has been solved, you must then choose your hotel with great care. It's a big investment to make, so be sure to examine the following points:

1. *The area.* What is the competition like? Are there any plans for re-development locally which might involve one of the big hotel groups? Is it on a main road or tourist route, or is it hidden in the back streets or down a country lane? Does the area as a whole seem to be coming up in the world, or going down?

2. *The customers.* Ideally, you want to attract a variety of clientele, so that you are fairly busy all year round. Sea-side hotels are full up for most of the summer, but virtually deserted in the winter — are you going to make enough profit to cover those lean winter months? Other hotels in industrial or commercial areas will find that they are full of business-men during the week, but that the weekends are very quiet. The most successful hotels are those which have a good mix of commercial, holiday, conference and banqueting business. Study the accounts and see what the pattern of business is.

3. *The fabric.* What state is your hotel in? You must find out how much renovating or decorating needs to be done and how much this is going to cost. What are the maintenance costs likely to be?

4. *The Law.* There are a number of laws that the hotelier is subject to, including the Race Relations Act. One of the most important, if you are opening a new hotel, covers licensing. There are various guides to the licensing laws, but if you have to apply for a new licence, it is wise to do it through a solicitor.

Also very important is the Fire Precautions Act. Every hotel, if it sleeps more than six people, must have a fire certificate from the local fire authority. When buying a going

153

concern, find out if it has a fire certificate, or if an application for one has been made (if not, the hotel is being run illegally). If the fire authority has already inspected the building, check on the cost of any alterations required to bring the premises into line with the Fire Precautions Act, 1971.

5. *Staff.* Good staff are obviously essential for the smooth and efficient running of a hotel, but unfortunately they are very difficult to come by. This is an industry with a very high staff turnover, especially among unskilled staff, and you must expect to spend a lot of time interviewing, supervising and training. Everyone in the business agrees that it pays to take your time (however inconvenient) and select staff very carefully, rather than always employing the first person you see because you are busy.

Training

For those who want to train for a career in hotel management, there are various degree and college courses, as well as courses run in conjunction with the Hotel and Catering Industry Training Board (see Useful Addresses).

Letting rooms

The mass of legislation which now covers the private letting of accommodation has made the business of being a landlord less and less worthwhile, with the result that many landlords are now selling out and putting their money elsewhere. This is a pity as there will always be a demand for cheap, short-term furnished accommodation, and it looks as though the supply is now drying up.

Legislation

The basic principle introduced by the Rent Act (1974) is the abolition of the old distinction between furnished and unfurnished property, in so far as this affects security of tenure. *All* tenants, either of furnished or unfurnished accommodation, where the landlord does not live in the house are 'protected' under the Act: this means that they cannot be given notice to quit except under certain very specific circumstances, such as repeated non-payment of rent. There *are* certain exceptions, the most notable one being the exemption from the requirements of the Act which is extended to landlords letting rooms in their own homes. Exemption may also be extended to landlords providing a 'service' such as breakfast or cleaning, but it would be unwise to think that such a provision would automatically provide a loophole. If you are planning to let a property, and you yourself are not planning to live on the premises, you must bear in mind that it could be extremely hard to get rid of undesirable tenants, and, moreover, that the rent initially asked may be reduced by the Rent Officer. If you are letting rooms in your own home, the relevant legislation is less stringent, but you may still have problems.

Finance

Interest rates are now generally so high that interest on loans almost equals gross returns, before tax, repairs, rates, etc have been paid, so you will have to consider the financial viability of the proposition very carefully.

Selection of tenants

If you still want to go ahead, a major consideration will be the selection of suitable tenants, since you may be stuck with them for a long time. Foreigners are now being sought out as tenants, as landlords (rightly or wrongly) feel that they are not likely to stay very long. Students are also likely to be transient. Your main criteria, though, should be the reliability of the prospective tenant, and the likelihood that he will take reasonable care of your property. You should always ask for references from a bank or an employer, and a damage deposit.

Furniture/dividing the house into units

If you have a whole house to let, you will need to decide whether to let furnished or unfurnished, and whether to let the house as a whole, or to divide it up into flats or bedsits. If you decide to let furnished, you have additional expenditure, but will be able to charge more rent. Much of the furniture (things like chests, tables, wardrobes) you should be able to pick up second-hand at auctions or sales, but it is a good idea to buy essentials, such as beds, new. The question of whether to divide the house up into units depends very much on the type of tenant that you have in mind, but it is becoming more and more usual to let houses as complete units to groups of students or young people. One or two of them sign the lease, the others are sub-tenants. The advantage to the landlord of this arrangement is that he has far less work to do: he only has to collect the rent from one person, rather than several, and only one person contacts him with regard to repairs, etc. He also does not need to arrange for the cleaning and upkeep of 'common' areas such as stairways and bathrooms. There is just one point to watch. If you do run into trouble, the law on joint tenancies is very complicated, so it would be wise to consult a solicitor before you enter into such an arrangement of letting *en bloc* to numbers of people.

Repairs

It is advisable to find a reliable odd-job man and employ him to carry out running repairs. To save yourself time you could arrange for the tenants to contact him, pay him and then forward the bill on to you. Some tenants will want to decorate their own rooms, and you should make it very clear to them at the outset whether you will allow this or not: it is probably a good idea to let them go ahead, and even offer to pay for the materials, since it will save you the trouble of doing it and they are unlikely to make the place completely uninhabitable. Under the Rent Acts internal decoration is usually seen as the tenant's responsibility anyway.

Tenants in your own home

If you are thinking of letting rooms in your own home, you should consider very carefully the effect this is likely to have on you and your family. Tenants are unlikely to keep the same hours as you, and you will have to put up with a certain amount of disturbance if they come in after you have gone to bed, or if they are coming and going while you have visitors. They will either need cooking facilities, which may result in confusion in the kitchen, or cook in their own rooms, which means cooking smells upstairs and stains on the carpets. If you are providing breakfast and/or other meals, your wife will have a great deal of extra work and your family life will be disrupted to some extent.

Rents

For guidance on the level of rents to expect in your area, consult your local Rent Officer. If you are a resident landlord, it is the Rent Tribunal which determines a fair rent. The local Council will keep a list of rents fixed in the Borough which you can consult.

Pubs

The following section refers to brewery tenants, not to pub managers (who are not self-employed) or to the owners of free houses, which are now so few and far between as to make the possibility of finding a vacant one very unlikely.

Tenants rent their pubs from the brewery company, paying an agreed sum to the outgoing tenant for fittings, equipment and stock. They agree to buy their beer from the brewery, and generally cannot buy stock (even of items other than liquor) from any other source without the brewery's permission. They keep their own profits and are responsible for their own losses, the brewery receiving only the rent on the premises and the guaranteed outlet for its product.

There are more applications from prospective tenants than there are tenancies available, so the breweries are able to 'pick and choose' to some extent. The qualities they look for in a prospective tenant are:

1. Sufficient capital resources to purchase fittings, equipment, and stock in hand, to cover immediate running expenses, and to provide a sufficient reserve to cover the tenant in the event of a temporary fall-off in trade.
2. Married tenants are preferred. A helpful and enthusiastic wife is important — running a pub is very much a family affair, and the wife's experience and attitude can be a deciding factor.

3. Good health, since running a pub involves hard physical work and long hours.
4. Some managerial experience, in any trade, would count in the applicant's favour, though it is not strictly necessary. Similarly, experience or training in the liquor trade would be useful, though again it is not a mandatory requirement.

Tenancy agreements

Most breweries have a standard form of agreement to be signed by the tenant. The procedure for taking over the fittings, furniture and equipment is the only area in which there may be a substantial difference between breweries: some require that the new tenant buys these items from the outgoing tenant, whilst in other cases they remain the property of the brewery, and the tenant lodges a deposit, returnable when he gives up the tenancy. Other items covered in the tenancy agreement include rent (usually paid quarterly), the term of the tenancy, responsibility for repairs, a requirement that the tenant take out employer's and public liability insurance, the terms on which the stock is purchased, the brewery company's right of access to the premises, requirements connected with transfer of the licence, and terms on which the tenancy can be terminated.

Licences

The tenant usually takes over premises that are already licensed, so he has to negotiate the transfer of the licence from the outgoing tenant to himself. It is advisable to be represented by a solicitor in your application for transfer of the licence.

Training

If you are accepted by a brewery for a tenancy, and neither you nor your wife have any experience of the trade, it is likely that both of you will be asked to attend a short residential course, run by the brewery company and lasting from one to two weeks. Whilst you are waiting for a suitable tenancy, or applying to different breweries, it is advisable, if you have no experience, to work part-time in a pub — this will give you some experience, and will help you to decide whether you are really suited to what is in fact a very arduous job.

Restaurants

New restaurants, especially in the London area, open every week. Despite the economic squeeze there still seems to be a great demand for this service and it will continue to be profitable for those with the necessary flair.

There are basically two kinds of people who open a restaurant — the gifted amateur and the professional. The gifted amateur is probably a superb cook who has been persuaded by his friends to lavish his talents on a wider public. His main problem is likely to be how to maintain standards without wasting an enormous amount of food and losing money. One answer is to have a *small* choice of dishes which are changed regularly, otherwise large quantities of coq au vin may end up in the dustbin because no one fancied it that week. He will also have to spend quite a lot of time finding the best sources locally for fresh meat, fish and vegetables, since his reputation depends on it. The restaurateur who has a speciality (such as steaks) and sticks to it will find life a lot simpler.

The professional will either have taken a full-time college or even degree course (see *British Qualifications*) or else trained in the kitchens of one of the great hotels, supplemented by part-time classes. High-fliers could also attend one of the European hotel schools or do a course at the Cordon Bleu Cookery School.

The professional will obviously have a much better idea of how to plan menus, avoid waste, manage a freezer, etc, but when it comes to running a business the problems are likely to be the same, however qualified you are.

Where your restaurant is located is obviously essential. If it is in the centre of town, well and good. If not, you must set about advertising, make sure your friends spread the word around, find an eye-catching décor and try to get yourself written up in the local paper. If you are sufficiently confident, you could try writing to the restaurant critics on some of the big magazines (such as *Harpers/Queen*) or newspapers.

If your restaurant is quite small, you will probably find it more economical in the long run to be as mechanised as possible with chip machines, dishwashers, freezers, etc, rather than hiring a lot of expensive, possibly unreliable, staff. Costing can be quite difficult, with the rising price of food, but beware of undercharging. There is a temptation to court trade with low prices, but you will soon find it impossible to keep up standards. It is a good idea, too, to realise your limitations and not try to be grander than you are — if you are basically steak and chips there is no point in trying to produce Cordon Bleu-type menus: you will soon be found out!

Retailing

The following guidelines apply to small retail businesses in general; details of specific *kinds* of shops are given on pages 164 to 165.

Buying a shop

You can either buy an existing business or build a new one up from scratch. Either way, you will want to make a careful investigation of locality, potential, future profits in relation to capital outlay, etc, before you commit yourself.

Buying an established business

Shops for sale are sometimes advertised in the local and national press and in trade journals, or you can consult a firm of business valuers and transfer agents. It is a good idea to write down the specific requirements that you are looking for: this will not only help you to brief your agent and any other advisers such as your accountant and bank manager, but will also help you clarify your ideas.

Shops are generally rented on a leasehold basis, and you have to pay for fixtures and fittings, existing stock, and 'goodwill'. (If the shop is bought freehold, this obviously gives much greater security of tenure but also involves a much higher capital investment.) How this price is arrived at depends on a number of factors, which you must analyse carefully before you commit yourself. *Stock* is generally valued for business sale purposes at current market cost price, and an independent valuation of the stock is desirable. *Fixtures and fittings* should also be independently valued, and an inventory of these should be made and attached to the contract of sale. 'Goodwill' is a nebulous concept to which an exact value cannot be attached. Obviously, the more the shop relies on regular, established customers, the higher the value of the goodwill; conversely, the more it relies on casual, passing trade, the lower the goodwill value. The price of a shop will also to a large extent depend on the potential of the local area. You will need to make a careful assessment of factors such as:

1. Competition. Don't make the mistake of thinking that the absence of a nearby competitor *necessarily* guarantees success. A shop that has done reasonably well in the face of nearby competition is a safer bet than a shop with a similar record which has had a virtual monopoly of local trade. There is always a danger that if there is no competition, someone else may move in after you. Another common mistake is to see only shops of the same trade as competition. Indirectly, all other traders in the area are competition, since all are competing for a share of the consumers' spending power.
2. Nearness to railway stations, bus stops etc : this may substantially increase the flow of passing trade. A map may help to clarify the exact potential of the location.
3. Any future local development plans — check with the local authority.

As mentioned in Chapter 9, it is also important that you and your accountant study the books thoroughly. In particular, examine the trend of the profit and loss account over the past few years to determine whether the business is improving. Another important point to note is whether the previous trader has been paying himself a salary, or whether this has to be deducted from the net profit figure.

Starting from scratch

You may want to take over premises which have previously been used for other purposes, in which case you should look closely at the previous owner's reasons for closing down and determine to what extent the same factors will affect you, even though you are engaged in a different trade. If you are going to use them for another type of business, you must get planning permission first. Or you may want to rent newly built premises, in which case you will probably have to pay a premium. The premium is based on the potential of the area, but try to get some *exact* idea of what that potential is: the number of new flats being built nearby, for example. In general, the premium should be lower than the goodwill price you would pay for a going concern, since it only indicates potential, not a record of success.

Further reading

Buying a Shop, written and published by E A Jensen, 39 Withdean Crescent, Brighton, Sussex.

Running a shop

Stock

It is sensible to buy your stock from a wholesaler, a cash and carry or from a manufacturer's agent, since you will generally need frequent deliveries of small quantities of goods. Have as few sources of supply as possible, to cut down your workload. There are a few exceptions to this — in the case of cigarettes, for example, it is better to deal directly with the manufacturer.

Make sure you know at all times what your stock levels are, and devise a system whereby you know when to re-order, before stocks run too low. The stock should be cleaned and dusted regularly and any stock that remains unsold over a long period should be discarded. Stock-taking should be carried out at least once a year.

Layout and display

Try to keep the layout of the shop flexible, and use space as efficiently as possible. Make the interior of the shop as attractive as you can: displays, however small, should have a focal point, and should be changed frequently. You may want to hire a freelance window dresser occasionally.

Security

Never leave cash lying about. If there is a lot of money in the till, take out a round sum in notes and leave a chit in the till to remind yourself where it is. Watch out for shoplifters, and ensure against them as far as possible by not leaving small, valuable items in easily accessible positions. Do not leave customers or visitors unattended. Remember that you must be insured right from the start, even before you have opened up for business.

Legal obligations

The most important Acts affecting shops are:

Contracts of Employment Act
Offices, Shops and Railway Premises Act
Shops Act
Trade Descriptions Act
Weights and Measures Act
Sale of Goods Acts
Local Authority By-laws
Consumer Credit Act
Redundancy Payment Act
Payment of Wages Act
Employment Protection Act
Sex Discrimination Act
Health and Safety at Work Etc Act

Get in touch with your local Shops Act Inspector before you begin trading. Your local Weights and Measures Inspector will also be of help.

VAT

For information on VAT see page 114

For further information

Contact The National Union of Small Shopkeepers of Great Britain and Northern Ireland. The Small Firms Information Centres produce a booklet *Starting a Retail Business* and have a reading list covering other aspects of the retail business. For addresses see pages 226 — 227.

Antique shops

Whether you are starting off from scratch or buying an established business, you will need funds to buy your initial stock. If you are inexperienced, and buy a going concern, you may find that the stock consists of all the duds and non-sellers of the previous owners, and you will have to get rid of it all and start again. If you are keen to acquire this particular shop it might be worth the risk, but otherwise ask a friendly dealer to look over the stock and give his opinion of its worth.

In any case, if you are inexperienced you must be prepared to spend some time 'getting your eye in' — and be resigned to the fact that you will make mistakes. Most dealers can tell a story of selling some apparently worthless item for a song, and then finding out its true value later — when the lucky buyer was miles away. But the positions will soon be reversed, especially once you have had some experience at the salerooms and found out what the foreign dealers are looking for. It is up to you then to keep your eyes open.

You must learn the technique of buying things at auctions —always go to the preview first and mark on your catalogue the items you are interested in and the price you are prepared to pay. Beware of being 'trotted' — other dealers running up the bidding and then dropping out at the end leaving you to pay an unrealistic price. Country auctions are usually widely advertised in local papers and you will soon get to know other dealers and their specialities. Dealers trade a lot with each other, and in fact many shops, especially in the south, make a good living from selling almost exclusively to foreign buyers.

You are most likely to make a success if you specialise, and learn as much as you can about your speciality, whether it is pictures, brass and copper, or china. Use *The Lyle Official Antiques Review* if at all in doubt about the auction value of any item.

One main drawback is the hours you will be expected to keep — this is *not* a 9 to 5 job! Evenings will probably be spent entering up sales, pricing new acquisitions etc, and then foreign dealers have a nasty habit of travelling overnight and arriving on the doorstep at 8 am ready to do business.

Bookshops

As mentioned earlier, the location of a bookshop is all-important when deciding what sort of books to stock: children's books, textbooks, hobbies, gardening etc. If you live on the tourist route it might be worthwhile stocking a lot of local history, while in another area it would be a good idea to find out what the local evening classes are.

You need to be devoted to your work, since you are going to work long hours, dealing with all sorts of queries from the public and some days you may be lucky to sell one Penguin book. What often makes a big difference is cultivating a connection with your local public library: if you can become their main supplier it will make a tremendous difference to your sales. School books are mainly bought centrally nowadays, but if there is a college in your area it is well worth finding out what textbooks are required and stocking a selection — you could even put a small ad in your window to that effect.

The antiquarian and second-hand book trade is extremely specialised and you really need to be an expert in the subject before you can hope to make any money in this area. People do make a lot of money, but they have to be prepared to invest thousands — they also need the patience to acquire the specialised knowledge needed.

Newsagents and tobacconists

Extremely hard work and long hours are involved in running this type of shop, and it is not a particularly profitable area. You will probably need to organise a daily delivery service for newspapers, which will involve getting up very early; you will have to deal with a large number of suppliers, whose representatives will be calling regularly; you will have all the headaches of VAT and the constant small price rises which particularly affect cigarettes and confectionery; and in addition to all this you will have to keep the shop open for as many hours as possible — most newsagents close only on Good Friday, Christmas Day and Boxing Day, the only days when newspapers are not printed. If your wife or another member of your family is available to work in the shop, the extra help will be invaluable, and you can avoid the problems which taking on staff might entail.

For further information, contact The National Federation of Retail Newsagents (see page 224 for address).

"I say I work for myself, but the truth is I work for the taxman."

High rates of tax are regarded as the curse of the self-employed, but with a personal pension plan they can be turned to good advantage.

You receive full tax relief on each annual premium – at the highest rate you pay, The Inland Revenue helps you to help yourself.

It's the tax-efficient way for the self-employed (or those who don't belong to a pension scheme) to save for their retirement.

Trident's Plan offers high benefits

The Trident Individual Pension Plan gives you a substantial tax-free cash sum at the time you retire, plus an income throughout your retirement – or you can dispense with the cash sum and opt for a considerably increased income.

Our example gives you an idea of just how high the benefits could be.

There are particular features, too, which help to make the Trident plan the obvious choice. For instance, the Trident plan is especially constructed to meet those two all-important needs – security and investment growth over the years.

If you want to make 1978/9 the year in which you start to pay less tax, send in the coupon for details.

For only £540 a year you could have a £6,000 p.a. pension plus a £19,000 lump sum.

Example: a 42 year old man paying tax at 40%

Here's how:

Your contribution	£900 p.a.
less tax saved	£360 p.a.
Your net outlay	**£540 p.a.**

(All for a net outlay over the years of less than £12.000)

Your benefits at the age of 65 (assuming a 10% rate of tax-free growth) could be:

The capital value	**£63,334**
This could provide	**£19,263**
lump sum free of all taxes	
	plus **£6,421 p.a.** pension

TRIDENT INDIVIDUAL PENSION PLAN

To: Trident Life Assurance Company Ltd., Renslade House, Whitfield Street, Gloucester GL1 1PG. Tel: (0452) 412785.
Please may I have details of your Individual Pension Plan.

Name _____
(MR/MRS/MISS)
Address _____

_____

_____ WFY 8/78 1PP

Trident Life

A Schlesinger Company

2: Providing a Service

We describe below some of the service industries, but there are obviously dozens more: window cleaning, office cleaning, launderettes, telephone-answering services, hairdressers, beauticians, careers advisers, tax consultants, nursery schools, driving schools, secretarial agencies, etc.

Some of these services require a fair bit of capital, since you are making a heavy investment in premises and equipment which must look attractive (eg hairdressing); but with others, where the client is unlikely ever to come to your office, there is no need for smart premises and expensive fittings.

To assess what the competition is like, look through the Yellow Pages in your local telephone directory. A lot of these industries are very much concentrated in the London area, but they are gradually spreading to the provinces and this is where you are most likely to find an opening: be the first person in the neighbourhood to open a launderette or a beauty parlour.

The building trades

bricklaying, carpentry, painting and
decorating, plastering

This section is primarily directed at people who want to undertake small jobs in private households, and does not concern itself with labour-only subcontracting on building sites.

Training

The orthodox training for these trades is by entering into apprenticeship after leaving school, but it is now also possible

167

for older people to learn these skills at Government Training Centres (details from your local employment office). Courses for manual trades last six months, after which there is a year's probationary period with an employer. Trainees are paid an allowance whilst taking the six-month course.

Much of the work available in private households consists either of very small jobs, such as putting up shelves or wallpapering, or conversion work, for which you must take into account the building regulations (see below) and you or the house owner should get planning permission if applicable. You will find that the wider the range of skills you can offer, the more you will be in demand, since one job might involve both carpentry and decorating, for example.

It is advisable to work with a partner, since you will often need help with lifting, holding tools, etc. You also will find that it is invaluable to have contacts who specialise in other, related trades, since you will often find that you cannot complete a job without the help of, say, an electrician. Contacts will also help you to find work, since they will get in touch with you to finish jobs that they themselves cannot complete.

The building regulations

Major structural changes must conform with the building regulations. If in doubt, consult your local authority (ask for the District Surveyor or Building Inspector). For further information, consult *A Guide to the Building Regulations* by A J Elder (Architectural Press).

Planning permission needs to be granted for external extensions exceeding 1300 cubic feet.

If the building you are working on is listed as being of historic interest there may be regulations against changing its external appearance — again, check with the local authority.

How to get work

As explained above, contacts in related trades are invaluable. You might also obtain subcontracted work from small building firms. Landlords are useful people to cultivate, as they often provide a great deal of this type of work.

168

Sources of information

1. The Department of the Environment publishes a leaflet called *How To Find Out: getting the best from building information services*, listing 80 important information sources for the construction industry. They also publish a large number of advisory leaflets on subjects such as *Emulsion Paints*, *Frost Precautions in Household Water Supply*, *Sands for Plasters*, *Mortars and Renderings*, etc. These are available from HMSO bookshops or from *Building Centres* and other booksellers.

2. There are 13 *Building Centres* in different regional locations. The address of the London branch is 26, Store Street, London WC1. The other branches are at Belfast, Birmingham, Bristol, Cambridge, Coventry, Dublin, Glasgow, Liverpool, Manchester, Nottingham, Southampton, and Stoke on Trent.

3. The Building Research Establishment is the largest and most comprehensive source of technical advice available to the construction industry. It operates from three centres — Watford, Birmingham and Glasgow. (For addresses see p 220.)

Catering

A freelance cook can find plenty of work catering for small social functions such as church gatherings or club meetings, as well as private functions such as dinner parties. Simple buffet catering for small gatherings of up to 50 people or dinner parties for up to 20 guests can be managed single-handed: a team of several caterers, of course, could handle larger functions.

The key to successful catering on a small scale is careful organising and planning. Costing is an important element in planning, and costs can be kept to a minimum by bulk-buying and eliminating waste. It is recommended that you work out your overall costs, taking into account overheads such as petrol, equipment, etc, and then add on a percentage for your own labour. Twenty-five per cent is reasonable. Careful timing and co-ordination, so that you don't find that the coffee is slowly getting cold while the last speech is still in progress, is also important.

Basic equipment

Equipment can be bought from cash and carry centres. Basically, you need a large urn for making tea, at least four really large saucepans, three large teapots, and a couple of large jugs. To save washing up, it is often possible to use paper plates and cups, but it is a good idea to buy your own cutlery. You will also need some form of transport — preferably a van rather than a car.

Food

Food can be bought in bulk from cash and carry centres. Keep everything simple. Do not take on elaborate menus or complicated dishes until you have mastered the organisational problems involved in catering for groups.

How to find work

Contacts can be made through church organisations, local social clubs, etc and direct mail or the local paper is a good way of advertising your services.

Cleaning

Cleaning, traditionally low-paid, unskilled work, can be a useful 'filler-in' for people in unreliable, chancy professions such as acting or modelling. Its great advantage is that work can often be obtained at very short notice and then dropped once something more lucrative comes up.

However, if one is prepared to swallow one's pride to some extent and take up cleaning on a full-time, permanent freelance basis, it can be quite interesting, though not particularly rewarding in financial terms, as it can lead to contact with a wide variety of people.

How to get work

Local advertising, once again, is one of the traditional

methods of finding domestic cleaning work. Personal contacts and local women's organisations are another source. Domestic cleaners are usually in great demand, so you should not have any problems.

You may prefer to do office cleaning, in which case you should telephone small offices and ask for work, or advertise in the local paper.

Agencies

Setting up your own cleaning agency is a relatively straightforward affair, since you can initially do the cleaning yourself and then graduate to a purely administrative and coordinating role, taking on casual workers as and when the need arises. Cleaning agencies sometimes offer odd-job and babysitting services as well.

Rates of pay

Pay in london is usually £1 to £1.50 an hour, while in the provinces 60p to 80p is the going rate. Fares are often paid as well.

Disc jockeys

Most people start doing DJ work because they enjoy entertaining people and listening to music. Essential requirements for the DJ are a lively, outgoing personality, a good knowledge of pop music (some DJs specialise in one particular type of music) and as large a selection of records as possible.

Disc jockeys are engaged by clubs, pubs, etc, either on a regular basis or for one-off sessions. They are generally expected to bring their own records, but equipment may be provided.

Equipment needed

The minimum equipment needed to run a mobile disco is: a

pair of turntables, which must be fairly robust as they will
probably be knocked about quite a bit; an amplifier of at
least 100 watts, preferably more; at least two 50-watt
speakers; and some form of transport, preferably a van rather
than a car. With this basic equipment, you could play at
private parties of from 50 to 80 people, but you would
not be equipped to work in clubs, pubs or public halls of any
kind.

For the more ambitious, and those with more money to
invest, a magnetic cartridge, which improves the quality of
the sound, is recommended, and this involves the use of a
pre-amplifier and a mixer. You will probably want to use
more than two speakers, and a more high-powered amplifier.
You may want to invest in stereo equipment, although you
will find that this can create problems caused by the many
different kinds of rooms in which you will want to use the
equipment. Beyond basic equipment, you may decide to
provide 'extras' such as a light show, a microphone for the
DJ, a strobe, or even go-go girls, all of which can push your
costs up considerably.

Copyright and licences

If you are going to operate a mobile discotheque as part of a
public performance, which is defined as one which takes
place 'outside the domestic or home life of the participants',
then it is necessary to obtain a licence from Phonographic
Performance Ltd, 14-22 Ganton Street, London W1. Applications should be submitted in advance for each event or
series of events as licences are not automatically granted.
Phonographic Performance exists partly to protect the interests of musicians and for larger halls and venues they may
insist on the incorporation of live music into the evening's
entertainment. A licence is needed for *any* kind of public
performance: even a performance at a firm's dinner dance,
for example, would need to be covered. The fees for a licence
are on a sliding scale, depending on the amount of time and
size of audience for which it is granted. For explanatory
literature contact Phonographic Performance Limited.

Playing a record involves two copyrights: that of the
record company, which is covered by the licence from
Phonographic Performance, and that of the music publisher
and composer, which is covered by the Performing Right
Society Ltd, 29 Berners Street, London W1. Most public halls

are covered by a licence from the Performing Right Society, but you should check up on this before operating in a public place.

Finding work

There are a large number of mobile discotheques operating, particularly in London and the Home Counties, so you will find that competition is keen. Demand tends to fluctuate seasonally, with November and December being the best months for bookings.

Advertising in local papers and magazines such as *Record Mirror* and the distribution of printed leaflets or business cards are recommended ways of getting bookings. DJs wanting to work in clubs or pubs usually find work through contacts or by going round and introducing themselves.

Pay

Variable, according to the type of function and equipment used. Mobile discotheques charge between £30 and £40 a night for private parties, more for weddings and public functions. You must 'cost' your time to a certain extent: if you are playing at a private party, for example, it is likely that you will have to carry on well after midnight, and you should allow for this.

Market research interviewing

Market research interviewing mainly involves either visiting people in their own homes to ask them their views about commercial products (or possibly about social issues) or stopping people in the street to ask them a series of questions about a particular subject.

Basic requirements for the job are patience, perseverance, and the ability to relate to a wide variety of different types of people. You must be available to work some evenings and weekends, and possibly to spend the occasional night away from home. A car is *not* absolutely necessary, although it does help; and you must be on the telephone.

173

Training and opportunities

A short training course is provided by the big, reputable market research companies. It is fairly easy to be accepted for a training course, as interviewers are generally in short supply — but it is important to show that you are going to be available for work on a long-term basis, as the company sees your training as an investment.

Most interviewers put their names down with several market research companies. They can expect a steady flow of work, particularly in London — probably less so in the rest of the country.

Opportunities exist for promotion from interviewing to supervisory and managerial posts, but after promotion one would no longer be working on a freelance basis. Other types of freelance work, besides interviewing, are sometimes available from market research firms: clerical work, for example, or the coding of questionnaires.

If you are interested in working as a market research interviewer, write to the Market Research Society who will supply on request a list of research companies employing interviewers. Or you can contact one of the bigger, more reputable market research agencies such as the British Market Research Bureau Ltd, or Research Bureau Ltd (see addresses on pp 219 — 227).

Pay

About £6 — £7 for a six-hour day, plus expenses. Pay can be higher for experienced interviewers.

Playgroup leaders

Playgroups cater for pre-school age children, and are usually run on a fairly informal basis, either by one woman in her own home (possibly with the help of a friend or neighbour), or, for larger groups, by several people using a public hall or similar premises.

No formal training is needed, but many local authorities now organise courses for playgroup supervisors, and the National Extension College (32, Trumpington Street, Cambridge CB2 1SQ) runs a correspondence course.

If you are planning to run a playgroup in your own home,

you must be prepared to invest a certain amount of money in sturdy, sound equipment (climbing frame, sandpit, painting equipment, constructional toys, etc.). You will need insurance, and you will have to make sure that your home meets the required safety standards — the Fire Officer will have to inspect your premises. You will also need planning permission, and you are legally obliged to register your playgroup with the local Department of Social Services.

Most of these requirements also apply to larger, hall-based groups, though you will probably not need to apply for planning permission, since most halls have permission for a variety of community activities which would include playgroups. Larger groups are often run by a committee consisting of the supervisor, at least one parent, the local health visitor, a secretary and chairman. Staff requirements for a large group (of, say, 25 children) would include a supervisor, one or two paid assistants, and 'mother-helpers' working on a rota basis.

Fees

These can be calculated by adding together total costs (wages, rent, insurance, a fund for equipment, day-to-day expenses such as postage, repairs, etc.) and dividing the total by the number of children that will be attending. If you find that the resulting fees are too high for local mothers to afford, then the playgroup can be subsidised by fund-raising activities such as fetes and bazaars. It will help you to cover your costs if you charge fees in advance, and it is also a good idea to charge an 'absentee' fee of half the normal rate for children who are unable to attend for short periods.

For further information, contact The Pre-School Playgroups Association (PPA) (see p 224).

Selling insurance

Selling anything calls for a lot of self-confidence, determination and perseverance. You have to be prepared to go out on the road and meet perfect strangers, chase up every contact, however vague, ring up firms that might conceivably be interested, and always be prepared for rebuffs, rudeness or just plain indifference. It helps if you have previously had a job that involves meeting lots of people, such as market research.

To get started, write to several of the big insurance companies. If you are accepted by one of them, you will be sent on a short (approximately two weeks) training course. After that, you are on your own, though of course most firms give a lot of guidance at first and may even send someone out with you on a few calls to give you a bit of confidence. You will be expected to work from home, though some companies do provide a desk and a telephone (otherwise you have to pay your own telephone bills). How much time you spend in the office with colleagues, picking up tips and discussing plans of campaign, is entirely up to you.

The various companies do operate slightly different systems of payment: some pay a salary, of varying size, in conjunction with commission, while with others you will be on a straight commission basis. It helps to have some money behind you while you are getting established, as it may take a while for the first cheque to come in.

Travel agency

Anyone can buy a shop and set up in business as a travel agent — you don't need any special licence or authorisation. On the other hand, if you want to become an authorised agent for British Rail, or any of the major airline companies, or for any of the big shipping companies, there is rather more involved. Before you can earn commission on the sale of tickets from these various bodies, you have to satisfy them that you are a reputable company; and their requirements can be fairly stringent.

Two essential requirements if you are setting up on your own are contacts inside the business and sufficient capital. Most people will acquire the necessary experience *and* the contacts by working in a big agency for a year or two until they have learned the ropes. At the same time they will probably work part-time for the examination of the Association of British Travel Agents.

Most reputable agents belong to the Association of British Travel Agents, who also have to be satisfied that you are a reputable firm. If you are a limited company, they require you to have an issued share capital of £5000 and also to put up another £5000 as a bond for your bank or insurance company. To gain the approval of IATA (International Air Transport Association) and British Rail (who all do their own, very thorough, investigations) you have to prove that you are a reputable firm with sufficient financial backing, that you are generating sufficient business to warrant selling their tickets (the financial requirements vary according to the locality), that your staff are sufficiently trained and knowledgeable, that your premises are of a sufficiently high standard and promote the right image. Then, and only then, will you be able to advertise that you are an authorised agent.

It will take at least one to two years to work up the necessary volume of business. In the meantime, most people concentrate on hotel bookings and package tours: you can deal in air and rail tickets, but only through another friendly agency, and of course *you* don't then earn the commission (it's illegal).

Choosing the right area is obviously important — centre of town, busy suburb, prosperous market town, for example. Remember, too, that the most lucrative business is done with firms: you should cultivate every contact you can find in the hope of becoming *the* company agency for nearby business firms.

Van and cab driving/light removals

If you can afford to invest in a reasonable, fairly large second-hand van, you can do light removals — something which is in great demand, particularly in the larger cities where the transient bedsitter population creates a constant demand for this kind of service. All that you need is a van and a telephone: a few advertisements in local shop-windows, recommendations from friends, and you are in business! This sort of work can easily be done on a part-time basis, as people moving flats are likely to want to move at weekends or in the evenings. If you want to work full-time, though, it might be worth setting up a partnership with two or three other van-owners, with a central office and a full-time receptionist to answer the telephone and arrange bookings. People wanting to hire a van for a couple of hours are likely to ring another firm if you are not in or cannot come at a particular time, but if you have a receptionist to allocate the work, three of you are each likely to get more work than any one of you could handle independently. A small van can also be used to handle small deliveries for private firms — distributing magazines, for example.

You should charge from the time you leave home until the time you arrive back (ie you include the time it takes you to get to and return from a particular job).

How to find work

Advertise locally. (One driver we talked to estimates that £1's worth of advertising would bring in £10—£20's worth of work.) It is also worth getting business cards printed, and leaving them with the customer after you have completed a job: they may ring again, or recommend you to friends.

Cab driving

Apart from orthodox taxi firms, who employ full-time drivers 'plying for hire' — ie to a large extent picking up fares on a casual basis in the street — there are also cab-hire firms who supply cars with drivers on demand, in response to a telephone call or some other kind of prior arrangement. These firms do not maintain a vehicle fleet of their own but employ outside people — generally part-timers — who drive their own cars, picking up the cab-hire firm's clients. The cab-hire firm thus acts in somewhat the same way as an employment agency — they supply the leads for drivers on their books.

To get this type of work you should have a clean driving licence and you must take out a special 'hire and reward' insurance.

Remuneration varies from place to place and from firm to firm, but like ordinary taxi fares it is based on the mileage, the time the job takes and the hour at which it is carried out. The cab-hire firm lays down the rates and a percentage of the fare has to be paid to them on each job, though there are some firms that make a flat weekly charge to drivers on their books.

Work is obtained initially by phoning in to base, which is obviously chancy. However, once you have established your status as a regular, many cab-hire firms will offer to lease to you or otherwise supply you with a two-way radio and this is a much more reliable way of keeping up the flow of jobs.

Cab driving involves working long hours in order to make an adequate income, and remember that you must allow for petrol, depreciation and insurance. However, the casual nature of cab-driving — you can more or less pick your own hours and days of work, provided you are thoroughly reliable when you *are* on the job — makes this a suitable occupation for those who are filling in time between their more usual work.

Cab-hire firms are to be found in Yellow Pages. Alternatively, your local garage may be able to advise you of good firms who are looking for drivers with their own cars.

3: Freelance Marketing of Your Skills

Freelance work is especially attractive to young people with few commitments, and to married women, less so to those with families to support, because of the element of risk involved. It can include either part-time work, done for a short time to raise extra cash; or it can be a full-time job.

Freelance work has several major advantages as opposed to full-time employment. Firstly, it offers a certain degree of flexibility and freedom. One is freed from the necessity of *having* to work from nine to five, from rush-hour travel, from having to 'create' work if you haven't really got anything to do, from being directly under your employer's supervision.

The second advantage is the possibility, though not the certainty, of high earnings. Taken on an hourly or weekly basis, freelance work is more highly paid than ordinary employment, though your pay doesn't include sick pay, pension contributions, holiday pay, the employer's National Insurance contributions, or payment for the almost inevitable slack periods which occur in most full-time jobs. From the employer's point of view, it is sometimes cheaper to use reliable freelances, as he doesn't have any commitments towards them. From the freelance's point of view, the main problem is ensuring that he or she has a continuing supply of work. Remember when calculating charges that you must allow for slack periods. However, given a continuing supply of work, freelance workers often make a lot of money. If a freelance charges £20 for a particular job, for example, the employer may think that he's had it done quite cheaply; what he doesn't realise is that there were two or three other £20 jobs in the same week!

The other major advantage of freelance work is that for tax purposes you are on Schedule D (self-employed) which

181

means that you can claim certain expenses against tax, and that your tax is paid at the end of the year, rather than on the PAYE system. For detailed information on taxation, see pages 101—116. There are a number of drawbacks to free-lance work, however. As we have already mentioned, there are slack periods. There is also the fact that you don't get holiday pay or sick pay, and that you have to buy your own National Insurance stamps (see page 103 for details).

For some people, though, the main drawback is the need for iron self-discipline. If you are at all inclined to put things off until tomorrow, you will probably find it hard to work as a freelance. Some people need the stability of a nine-to-five environment to get any work done at all; others (and these are the ones who turn out to be successful freelances) are quite happy to stay up all night working, if necessary, and will put in a tremendous effort to keep to deadlines. Remember that you need to put more effort into freelance work than into an ordinary job: if you aren't reliable, you won't get any more work. Reliability and efficiency and the willingness to drop everything if a really urgent job comes up, are absolutely vital; the other absolute necessity is that you should be on the telephone, so that you can easily be contacted when a job comes up.

How to start out

It is difficult to give general guidelines about how to start out as a freelance: there are so many different types of freelance work that it is very difficult to generalise. People often start by working on a part-time basis and then graduate to full freelance status. This provides them with some security whilst they establish themselves. Others may go into a field in which they have no experience, relying on savings to tide them over the first few weeks or months.

In the following chapter, in which some suggestions for the kinds of work which can be done on a freelance basis have been outlined, we have tried to give some indication of the ways in which you can find work. In some areas, advertising may pay off; for others it will be worse than useless. Much freelance work is obtained through personal contacts, and this is usually the most fruitful source. There are a few employment agencies and other bodies which operate in this area, and details have been given where appropriate.

Charges

One of the hardest problems facing you will be the all-important question of calculating your charges. Will you charge per hour, or per job? How much are other people charging for similar work? How much will people be prepared to pay you? A lot of freelance work is paid on an hourly basis, and you will probably want to start off by being paid by the hour, until you have some experience of calculating how long it will take you to complete a job. Otherwise, you may find yourself out of pocket, having initially quoted a low price and then finding that the work has taken you longer than you expected. However, if you intend to make a real career as a freelance, on a long-term basis, you should eventually aim to charge per job rather than per hour, as you will in the long run make more money in this way.

Where possible we have tried to give some idea of the hourly rates of pay for different kinds of freelance work, but pay does vary between different localities, so check up with other freelances if possible. Don't underprice yourself too much: you will get plenty of work, but will exhaust yourself trying to complete it. Better to do less for more money: but don't price yourself out of the market either!

Travelling time and expenses

There seems to be some dispute among freelances about whether to charge for the time spent travelling to collect and deliver work. If you are doing something like letter-typing, or small design jobs, you could spend up to 30 per cent of your time travelling around between different jobs, and obviously this is a complete waste of time, from your point of view, unless you are being paid for it. It is difficult to establish any general rule which applies to travelling time, but the following guidelines may help:

1. If you are being paid £1.50 per hour or less, it is reasonable to expect to charge for at least *some* of your travelling time and fares, particularly if a lot of your time is spent travelling.

183

Invoice   4/9/78

To: London Advertising Ltd
From: Jane Smith, 20 Norton Road, London NW10

For 5 hours typing at £2 per hour   £10.00
Expenses (purchase of postage stamps)   £2.00
                                          ―――――――
                                           £12.00

Weekly record of hours   *Invoice sent*

For London Advertising   ☑

Monday: 5 hours & £2 expenses (stamps)
Charge: £2 per hour

For Thames Press Ltd.   ☐

Tuesday: 10 hours
Friday: 7 hours
Expenses: £1.00 fares
Charge: £2.50 per hour

For Rev L Green   ☑

Wednesday: 8 hours
Charge: £1.00 per hour

Figure 9. *Typical invoice and weekly record of hours.*

184

2. If you are being paid more than this, or are doing jobs that take more than a week or so to complete, then it is not really fair to charge for travelling time.

3. If you choose to live a long way from your various employers (if you live in the country, for example and travel to town once a week to collect and deliver work) then it isn't reasonable to charge for the time it takes you to travel into town. Similar rules apply to expenses. If you have to buy a piece of equipment solely for a particular job, the expense can be passed on to the employer, but you cannot really charge for something that you use all the time, such as hiring a typewriter or buying paper.

Keeping records

For tax purposes, you need to keep a record of your invoices (a small duplicate book will do) and a record of your expenses. It is worth employing an accountant to help you with your tax return: he will save you more money than you have to pay him in fees. (See also Chapter 3.)

You may find it helpful to keep a record of the number of hours worked in each week and tick them off when they have been invoiced. Examples of a typical freelance's invoice and weekly record of hours are shown in Figure 9.

Antique dealing

You do not necessarily need to have a shop to be an antique dealer. Some people with the necessary expertise make a living buying and selling furniture, pictures, etc from home. Obviously, you cannot hold the amount of stock you would find in a shop, but there are quite a lot of advantages to trading in this way: the main one is that you need very little capital since you don't have the expense of buying and stocking a shop, with all the overheads, etc.

The dealer buys a few pictures, pieces of furniture or china at a time, probably from local auctions, and then finds a buyer. You will soon become known in the trade, especially if you attend auctions regularly. Most shops and dealers specialise and so are constantly buying things from each other. Many people find, too, that they can make a good living selling almost exclusively to the foreign dealers who regularly visit this country.

It is most important, if you are going to make a profit, to know how much to pay for the various items. Never attend an auction unless you have been able to go to the preview first. The preview is where you have the chance to examine articles closely for faults and flaws, mark your catalogue with the items you are specially interested in, and finally (and most important) decide the top price you are prepared to pay and mark it. The last point is most important, for otherwise you might be carried away by enthusiasm into paying far more than the item is worth — and bang goes your profit. If in doubt about how much to pay, consult the 'Bible' — *The Lyle Official Antiques Review*, which gives the auction price for everything (revised annually). You should aim to pay slightly *less* than the price quoted in Lyle in order to make a profit.

If you fail to find a buyer, whether among friends, contacts or other dealers, you can advertise in the local or national press (depending on the quality of the item) and if all else fails you can put it back into auction and try to get your money back.

You can specialise, too, in furniture or pictures that need to be repaired or renovated — naturally you will then expect to sell them at a much higher price. Repairing genuine antique furniture is obviously a job for the specialist craftsman, but you should have no trouble in stripping or mending pine furniture. If you know a dealer or collector who specialises in them, it is also worth having clocks repaired or pictures reframed and cleaned.

Crafts

Dressmaking

There are various types of dressmaking that can be done at home: outwork for the garment trade; running up made-to-measure clothes; repairs and alterations; and specialised work such as leather work, embroidery or crochet, which can be sold to boutiques or through mail order. 'Outwork' is repetitive and the pay is low: it is not recommended. Making clothes for friends and for customers brought in by advertisements and recommendations is much more interesting, though even here the rewards may not be high. The easiest type of work is when the customer presents you with a commercially produced pattern and fabric for it, so all you have to do is cut it out and sew it together. Making your own patterns, on the other hand, requires a fair amount of skill as translating a flat piece of paper into a three-dimensional garment is quite a complicated business. If you *do* know how to make your own patterns, then the customer can present you with a rough sketch, or even just a description, and you work from there.

If the customer doesn't present you with the fabric for the garment she may give you vague instructions and then be unhappy with your interpretation of them. A compromise could be for you to go shopping with her, to ensure that the chosen fabric is suitable and that sufficient quantities are bought. Thread, zips and trimmings can be bought at the same time. Alternatively, you could build up your own stock, by buying remnants and reduced lines, and offer the customer a choice from these.

It is important to have a fitting as soon as the garment is in one piece, and a second fitting may be needed to check on details such as the hang of a sleeve or to make sure that the collar lies flat.

Alterations (zips, hems, etc) form quite a high proportion of the work of many home dressmakers. These jobs can be fiddly and time-consuming, but it isn't possible to charge much for this type of work, so if you advertise your services you may find it worth your while to emphasise the fact that you don't want to do alterations.

Embroidered, leather or crochet garments can be sold to boutiques or by mail order (most women's magazines carry small ads for clothes). You must make sure that you have sufficient stock to cover any bulk orders you may receive. You also need a talent for sensing fashion trends almost before they happen, as it will take several months before your garments appear in the shops.

You really need an electric sewing machine: a swing-needle one will enable you to do zigzag stitches, useful for buttonholes, neatening off raw edges and simple embroidery. A zip foot for the machine is also desirable. Other pieces of equipment you will need are pins (buy new ones every year or so, as they eventually become blunt), shears, needles, thread (keep two or three reels of black and white in stock, and buy other colours when you need them), french chalk, a button-hole cutter (sometimes called a 'quick unpick' or 'seam ripper' — it is also used for unpicking seams), a tape measure and a steam iron.

As with other crafts, the usual way to learn is by taking evening classes or by reading and experimentation. There are a large number of books on dressmaking on the market, many of them illustrated with glossy photographs of the finished product: you may find, however, that books giving detailed diagrams of the sewing processes involved are more helpful.

Jewellery

The designing and making of jewellery is a highly competitive, cut-throat business. Before investing in expensive materials and equipment, you must prove to yourself that you have some flair for design and are suitably skilful with your hands. Starting off with lapidary work is a good way of finding out if you have the necessary artistic ability, and, most important, if anyone wants to buy your designs. From there, the best plan is to take an art college or City and Guilds course in jewellery, and sell the results while you develop some expertise (see *British Qualifications* for courses available). The great advantage of doing this is that you can use college equipment while you gradually build up your own collection of tools.

The most successful students find that they have no difficulty in selling their work while they are still at college. Start by showing off your handiwork to friends — if your work is good enough your reputation will spread by word of mouth and you will soon find the orders coming in. From there you can progress to taking samples of your work round the various jewellers and department stores in the hope of getting orders. You can also hire a stall in a street market on Saturdays and see how successful you are.

The initial outlay on tools can be quite small — £2 or so — if you are able to use college equipment as well. Eventually of course you will need your own equipment and this can be very expensive so you would be wise to save some of your initial profits towards buying equipment. Materials are also expensive. Jewels are bought from craft shops, while gold is bought from Hatton Garden — here again you will find it cheaper if you can prove you are attending college.

With such expensive materials it is obviously important to get the pricing right, if you are going to make a reasonable profit. Here your best plan is simply to show samples to a well-established jeweller. He will soon tell you how much he would charge, since he obviously does not want to be undercut by a newcomer.

Knitting and crochet

If you are a quick skilful worker, good at spotting fashion trends, you will probably be able to make a living making hats, scarves, sweaters, children's clothes etc. Buy the wool wholesale from one of the Yorkshire mills (they advertise in the women's magazines) and be prepared to spend all your free time slogging away. The quicker you are the better, of course. Take samples round the local craft and gift shops and suitable stall-holders in local street markets. If your work is really eye-catching and original, try some of the big department stores. Beware of landing too big an order — it would be marvellous if Liberty's ordered 200 sweaters, but would you be able to make them in time?

If you want to take on big orders, the best plan would be to find a few housebound housewives with the necessary skill who would be glad of some pocket money. You might even think of going into partnership with another knitter.

Knitwear firms are often on the lookout for women who can knit or crochet specialised merchandise, but be careful — they pay very low rates.

Knitting with a machine is a lot faster, and you might consider investing in a second-hand machine. ILEA runs knitting-machine courses — consult your local public library for courses in other areas.

How much to charge? You can price similar goods in the shops, but remember that the shop wants its cut too, so you will have to be content with less than the shop price. On the other hand people are usually willing to pay more for hand-made goods — if you charge too little, you'll have to slave away for hours and hours to make any money at all.

Lapidary work

Lapidary is the art of working in gemstones or pebbles and it forms an excellent introduction to the art of making jewellery, since the basic materials are not so expensive as in jewellery proper.

Learning the techniques of lapidary work is quite simple: there are lots of books on the subject, as well as clubs and societies. *Gems* is a monthly magazine which lists suppliers, as well as clubs and organisations. Most books will also give you a list of the tools and equipment required. The main item of equipment for lapidary work at home is a tumbler, costing approximately £25, though you may be able to pick one up second-hand through a club. The tumbler is used for grinding and polishing the stones (obtained from craft shops) which are then set in silver, copper, steel etc to make rings, pendants or brooches.

You will have to be patient — it can take up to 12 weeks to polish a consignment of stones. But you should then have no trouble selling your pieces via local shops, stalls in the local market, department stores, even coffee mornings. Don't undersell your work — have a look round the shops and see what comparable pieces fetch before offering your work to a shop.

Making loose covers and curtains

To make a living sewing, you must be an experienced needlewoman and a fast worker. Loose covers in particular involve far more work than the inexperienced would ever imagine — so don't gaily undertake to re-cover someone's sofa over the weekend. There are plenty of good handicraft books that give step-by-step directions, and provided you follow them accurately you should not have any problems, even as a beginner. The most important point with loose covers is to know how to measure up accurately — essential when dealing with expensive fabrics.

You will need a sewing machine with a piping foot, enough room to lay the material out properly for cutting and measuring, a really good pair of dressmaking scissors — and lots of patience.

Curtains, if they are to be done professionally, involve quite a lot of hand-sewing — an ideal job for anyone who is housebound.

You will soon find work by advertising in the local papers, and by word of mouth, once you have done a few jobs. To find out what to charge, ring up one of the big department stores that offer this service and ask them for a quote: make sure your quoted price is then a few pounds cheaper and you'll have no trouble finding more work.

Beware of taking on too much and so failing to deliver the goods in time. Take on one job at a time, until you know exactly how long it takes you to do a pair of curtains, or a chair cover, etc. Otherwise, you will end up with a lot of irate clients and a bad reputation for being unreliable.

Picture framing

ILEA run an evening course in picture framing. It is also possible to learn the craft by working in a gallery, though usually galleries are rather a 'closed shop'. Basically, as with all crafts, it is best to experiment as much as possible before you undertake commercial work.

You need a good work table and some large shelves on which to store your work.

Basic tools are:

A mitre saw for the corners
Clamps, to hold the corners together while they are being glued
Accurate rulers and a set square
Hammer and nails
A vice and mount cutter are useful, though not strictly necessary

Materials

Needed are mouldings, backing board, which can be either card or hardboard, and glass. Your local glass merchant will cut glass to the right size for you: this is easier than doing it yourself.

Suppliers are often unwilling to supply materials in small quantities, but if you look around, you should be able to find some small firms who are willing to do so. If you are keen on jumble sales, you will find that you can often pick up old picture frames for next to nothing, and these can be revamped.

For making the actual frames, great care and accuracy is needed in order to get the mitred edges to fit exactly. Step-by-step instructions for making different types of frames are given in *Framing*, by Eamon Toscano.

191

Compare prices by asking galleries and picture-framing shops for quotations.

Pottery

It is possible to 'teach yourself' by reading and experimentation, but if you want to take a course many local authorities run evening classes in pottery (they are popular so book as early as you can). In London, there is also an evening course run by Moonshine Community Arts Workshop, Victor Road, NW10.

Unless you are only going in for pottery in a small way, you will need plenty of space for working and storage. It is a good idea to convert your garage, or an outside shed, into a work room since it then won't matter if you make a mess. Your work room should ideally be equipped with a decent-sized sink, a solid work-surface, preferably with a plain wooden top, plenty of shelves, a damp cupboard (which can be a wooden cupboard lined with plastic sheeting or with slabs of plaster which are periodically soaked in water), and a waterproof container for storing clay. Other basic requirements are the kiln (if you are eventually planning on a high turnover of work, you will need to buy the largest kiln you can afford); the potter's wheel (though this is not absolutely necessary for a beginner, since you can do mould, slab and coil pottery without one); an assortment of bowls, buckets, basins, sieves, etc; and a set of small tools — cutting wire, a knife, scrapers, 'bats' (squares of hardboard used for carrying and drying pottery), sponges, brushes and modelling tools.

You may prefer to use your own local clay, in which case you will have to devote time to its preparation; or you can buy it ready-prepared from a potter's merchant or pottery supply house. Local brickworks will often supply clay cheaply, though it may need some extra preparation. It is usually supplied by the hundredweight, and smaller amounts are proportionately more expensive. It is important that it should be kept in a cool, damp place.

You can buy ready-made glazes, though it is possible to mix your own. You will also need sand, slow-setting potter's plaster, grog, oxides, slips (engobes) and wax.

Suppliers of equipment and materials

Harrison Mayer Ltd
Craft and Education Division
Meir
Stoke on Trent ST3 7PX

Mills and Hubball Ltd
Victoria Rise
Clapham Common
London SW4

Clay:

Potclays Ltd
Copeland Street
Stoke on Trent

Kilns:

Bernard Webber Ltd
Webcot Works
Alfred Street
Fenton
Stoke on Trent

A more detailed list of suppliers is given in *Simple Pottery* by Kenneth Drake, an excellent book which is recommended for the beginner.

If you visit craft shops with samples of your work, you will find that some will take pots on a sale or return basis, whilst others will buy a small quantity of your work outright and order more if it sells. Alternatively, you may want to sell your work direct to the customer, in which case you could start off by hiring a market stall (average price: £3 per day — steer clear of the most popular markets, which have long waiting lists) with the eventual aim of owning your own shop.

Upholstery

This is an area where it really pays not to price yourself out of the market. The real dyed-in-the-wool professional is so expensive that many people cannot afford the prices. If you have served a long apprenticeship you are of course entitled to charge the top rate; but if you are planning to work as you learn, set your sights a bit lower financially and you will find far more work. You can either buy junk furniture to do up yourself, or advertise to do up other people's furniture. Until you have had some experience, it is probably best not to invest too much money in buying furniture, unless you have lots of storage room and no immediate need for the cash.

The best way to start out is via evening classes: ILEA run classes in London. Otherwise, inquire at your local public library. There are plenty of good books on the subject, and you should soon be able to tackle bedroom or dining chairs, footstools, etc without any trouble, but don't attempt such things as buttoning, springs or chaise longues until you have had a bit more experience.

There is a tremendous demand for reasonably priced upholsterers, so you should not have much trouble finding work. Advertise in your local paper or even in the national press, once your work is good enough to tackle big pieces. It's also worth visiting a few antique shops — they often have upholstery jobs to be done.

The right tools are very important and not too expensive. You will need a webbing stretcher, tack hammer, set of upholstery needles and a regulator. You can buy the tools and materials (horse-hair, calico, cotton wadding, springs) from a specialist supplier — there are lots listed in the Yellow Pages.

Editorial work and indexing

For proof-reading and editorial work, experience in a publishing house is an essential prerequisite. People tend to feel that proof-reading, in particular, only requires a good command of spelling and an eye for detail, but in fact it really requires some knowledge of the way a book is actually put together, and an eye for the kinds of mistakes, such as incorrect spacing, that an inexperienced person (or the general reader, for that matter) would not necessarily pick up. It is most unlikely that an inexperienced person would be able to obtain freelance editorial work from any publishing firm.

However, if you have worked in publishing, you are quite likely to obtain freelance work through personal contacts. Forget the idea of advertising your services: it won't work.

Editorial work is in a way particularly suited to free-lancing: most of it can be done more quickly and thoroughly in the quiet of one's own home than in the distracting hubbub of an office atmosphere. (If you are working full-time in publishing, try suggesting this to your boss!) It also has the advantage of being time-consuming; once you have obtained a particular piece of work, you will usually find that it guarantees you one to two weeks' employment — and so you do not get into the situation in which some freelances find themselves, of having to spend up to half your time collecting and delivering work.

Indexing

The Society of Indexers (see page 225 for address) operates a scheme for *Registered Indexers* for those with experience in the profession.

Film extras

There isn't a great demand for film extras and the few people who do make a regular living out of it have generally been in the business for years. The work is irregular, the summer months generally being the most profitable.

Experienced extras usually have a large wardrobe containing a dinner suit, an Ascot suit and often their own police uniform. They are paid more for providing their own costumes.

To work as a TV extra, you must be a member of Equity. To work as a film extra, you needn't belong to Equity, but you must join the Film Artistes' Association (see p 000 for address). All bookings for extras in feature films within a sixty-five mile radius of London are handled by Central Casting Ltd (see p 000). If you want to work as a film extra you should apply to them, although they emphasise that they only consider a small proportion of the hundreds of applications they receive, and they provide no guarantee of work to those who are successful in registering with them.

The basic fee for a crowd artiste (an ordinary extra, as opposed to a stand-in or a double) is £15 per day, more if you provide your own costume.

Home typing/secretarial work

This kind of work is obviously well suited to married women

who wish to work from home. Little capital investment is needed — obviously one's own typewriter is necessary, but a second-hand, electric typewriter can be hired for around £40 per month, or bought for about £200 upwards (depending on the model). Obviously, no one is going to make a fortune doing typing at home, but the skilled typist may be able to make more money at home than in the average secretarial job, provided she can find sufficient work to do. There are certain pitfalls to be avoided, such as envelope typing, which is notoriously underpaid, but on the whole this is an area in which it is possible to make a reasonable amount of money, and which has the advantage of being flexible enough to fit in with domestic commitments.

How to find work

Classified advertisements are one source: authors sometimes advertise for people to type their manuscripts, for example. However, you will probably do better to insert your own classified advertisements in selected newspapers such as *The Times* and the *Daily Telegraph*, offering to type manuscripts, theses, etc. Another good place to advertise is the trade press, particularly if you have experience of doing secretarial work in a specialised area. Local advertising in shop windows, local newspapers and magazines might also be effective, as people requiring your services would have the advantage of knowing that you were close at hand.

It is perhaps better, though, to contact potential employers directly. People such as clergymen, MPs, doctors and architects, and various clubs, associations, etc often require part-time secretarial services, which can easily be provided from home. For this kind of work, it helps if you can do audio-typing, as you can then collect tapes and take them home, rather than having to take shorthand dictation.

Rates of pay

Pay for home typing is around £1.25 per hour, more if you are particularly skilled. Thesis and manuscript typing is sometimes paid according to the number of words typed, with a fixed charge per 1000 words. If you are doing this kind of work, and your typing is fast, it is probably more profitable to charge a fixed fee per thousand words. For letter typing, however, an hourly charge is probably preferable. Remember to keep an accurate record of the number of hours worked, and include the time that you have to spend collecting and delivering work.

Running your own typing agency

The employment agency field no longer offers the kind of opportunities it once did, as many large firms have moved into the area. However, there is one type of agency, admittedly limited in scope, which is a reasonable proposition for the independent operator. This is the small envelope typing and direct mail agency. You contact firms which do a lot of their business by sending circulars out to people, offering to handle their whole distribution — typing of envelopes or labels, inserting circulars into envelopes, and postage. The administrative work for this kind of business can easily be handled by one person (from their own home if convenient) and the actual mechanical work of envelope typing and stuffing can be farmed out to outworkers. Caution: Don't take on this kind of 'homework' yourself; you will probably be grossly exploited and underpaid.

IBM typesetting

If you are a *very* good typist, one of the most interesting and worthwhile possibilities for freelance work would be IBM typesetting. A high degree of skill is needed, and a fairly large investment, but this area offers far greater potential for high earnings and job involvement than straightforward typing.

The job involves preparation of typed matter which will eventually be printed photographically. Many small magazines, advertisements and books are now produced in this way, rather than by traditional letterpress printing.

The matter to be printed is typed out on a highly sophisticated golf-ball typewriter, capable of 'justifying' (making all the lines the same length) and producing copy which is similar in every respect to that produced by normal printing.

Obviously, if you are going to type this kind of work, your typing must be very, very accurate (although the odd mistake can be pasted over). You also need to know a certain amount about printing, proof correction marks, etc. However, the

197

techniques involved are basically the same as those needed for ordinary typing.

The best way to get involved in this area would be to gain some initial experience by working for a small typesetting firm, before setting up on your own. You would quickly be able to learn the techniques involved, and could then buy your own second-hand machine and work for yourself from home. As you could charge £2.50 upwards per page for your work, the investment would be well worthwhile. Work can be obtained from small publishing firms, design consultants, advertising agents, etc.

Modelling

All kinds of people, young and old, beautiful and ugly, are needed as photographic models for advertisements, posters, etc. The main requirements are self-confidence, poise, and a reasonably well-stocked wardrobe; but most important of all, your face and figure must be just what the photographer wants at the time.

The work can be very varied, involving short bookings lasting an hour or so, or location sessions lasting several days. You must be prepared, sometimes, for long delays whilst equipment and props are arranged, so you must have a reasonable degree of patience; it is also important that you should be absolutely punctual and reliable.

A lot of the opportunities for photographic models are in London, but it is possible to obtain modelling work in the provinces, particularly fashion modelling.

How to get work

The first step is to find an agent: look in Yellow Pages under 'Model Agencies'. You can also make direct approaches to photographers: look in Yellow Pages under 'Commercial and Industrial Photographers'.

Once you are registered with an agent, get him to recommend a photographer, and have some sample pictures taken. These will form the basis of a composite, or montage, of the model's best pictures, printed on two sides of a single sheet or on four sides of a small folder. The composite also shows details of the model's measurements, colour of hair, etc. You need to have at least 250 copies of the composite printed, as these will be one of your chief means of publicity.

If you have any special abilities or skills such as horse riding or skating, for example, and you possess the clothes to go with them, or if you have an old uniform (police, or the Forces), mention this to the agent — it may help you to get more work.

Fees are usually paid through the agent, who deducts commission — normally 15 per cent of any modelling fee. Avoid agents who ask for a registration fee before taking you onto their books.

Fashion modelling

So far we have referred to photographic modelling generally, but for many young people wanting to enter the business 'modelling' means 'fashion modelling'. Much of this is photographic work for magazines, but the actual display of clothes at fashion shows is also involved, and this type of work can be steadier and more reliable.

Aspiring fashion models need to be slim (34-23-34 or less) and the ideal height is about 5' 8". There are a number of modelling schools, and opinion seems to be divided as to their usefulness. But it is important that you get an accurate and honest assessment of your prospects before you spend any money on training or photographs. Reputable schools such as the Lucie Clayton Fashion School will do this anyway, and will not enrol students who have no chance of success, but there *are* a number of less scrupulous establishments, so beware.

For further reading

Jean Campbell Dallas, *How To Become a Photographic Model* (see bibliography).

Photography

As in other fields, in freelance photography you are more likely to succeed by organisation, reliability and perseverance than by sheer talent alone. If you are submitting samples of your work to magazines, journals and newspapers you must expect to have a large proportion of your work rejected; but on the small proportion that *is* accepted you can gradually build up your reputation with your clients.

Don't be misled by camera fanatics — it is important, of course, to have good, reliable equipment, but you don't necessarily need the most expensive, up-to-date gadgets and accessories to be a successful professional photographer. Far better to have sound, reliable equipment which you are happy with and you *know* that you can take good pictures with, and to take great care with the presentation of your work.

How to get work

Freelance photography covers such a wide area that it is difficult to cover all the possible avenues of entry to the profession. One fact stands out: there are a great many competent photographers, and so to be successful your pictures will have to have some special quality that makes them stand out, not necessarily in terms of technical proficiency but in terms of ideas. If you are trying to break into the women's magazine field, for example, it is no good taking along a portfolio of photographs which are almost exactly the same as the ones the magazine uses already; they know photographers who can produce these, and you must give them a very good reason for using you, as opposed to people they already know and trust.

Commissioned work

Most of the larger magazines commission work, for which the photographer is paid on a fee basis. Standard practice for obtaining commissioned work is the submission of a portfolio, backed up by one or more personal visits, and it is likely that your personality and ideas will carry more weight with the art editor than your technical expertise, though of course you must be technically competent.

Submitting work 'on spec'

It is possible to make a living by submitting selections of prints to magazines 'on spec', particularly if you concentrate on small, specialised publications and local magazines and newspapers.

Presentation of your work is very important. Prints should be of the highest quality possible, and should be carefully packed to avoid damage by the Post Office. Your work should be clearly labelled, and it is a good idea to have a referencing system, allotting a reference number to each photograph, to avoid confusion.

You should offer 'single reproduction rights': this means that the print can be re-sold at a later date, and you yourself retain the copyright.

Wedding photographs, passports, portraits

This area is one of the most attractive to people who want to make extra money from photography on a part-time basis, possibly graduating to full-time freelance work when they have established themselves. Work can be obtained through local advertising and personal contacts, and your local camera club should be able to give help and suggestions.

Payment

Rates of pay vary tremendously, since the work itself is so varied. Fees for commissioned work for the high-circulation women's magazines can be substantial, but most of this work goes to established photographers.

It is important to remember when dealing with magazines that payment may be delayed by as much as six months, and if you try to push for early payment you may make yourself very unpopular. It is unlikely, in any event, that you will be paid before publication. If you are going to be a full-time freelance photographer therefore, you shouldn't under-capitalise yourself, as it may be a year or so before you really begin to make enough money to live on.

Selling produce

Anyone who has a big enough garden or allotment can make money selling produce: flowers, fruit, vegetables, herbs, honey, home-made jams and chutneys and eggs. If you live on or near a main road the easiest way to sell things is simply to put up a stall or barrow at your gate, or else a notice directing people to your house. If you live right off the beaten

201

track you might find it easier to sell to your village store or to one of the 'farm shops' that are to be found now in many villages. In the summer you can make a lot of money from passing trade — tourists and city dwellers on the lookout for country produce — while in the winter you are more likely to be selling to commuters and weekenders who have not got time for gardening.

Two worthwhile investments, when you have made enough money, are a deep freeze and a greenhouse. With a deep freeze, you can freeze surplus fruit and vegetables to sell in the winter, or for people to transfer to their own freezers. This enables you to make a bit more money in the lean winter months. With a greenhouse, you can grow some of the more exotic vegetables such as green peppers and aubergines, grow potted plants, especially for the Christmas trade, and offer bedding plants such as tomatoes to other gardeners.

How much should you charge? A quick scout round the local shops will tell you what the going rate is for the more usual fruit and vegetables. You should of course charge more than shop prices for home-made jams, jellies and chutneys. The price of eggs varies with the time of year, but again you can check with your local store — remember you can charge more for 'free-range' eggs, provided they *are* free-range.

Teaching/tutoring

If you have a degree, teacher's diploma or some other qualification it is worthwhile thinking about private coaching, especially if you have children of your own and perhaps find it difficult to work normal school hours. Try advertising in your local paper or, better still, in the personal columns of *The Times*, *Daily Telegraph* or *The Times Educational Supplement*. State the subjects you are prepared to teach, and the level. Demand will depend a lot on the area in which you live: you might do better in the 'smarter' areas where parents tend to worry more about their children's education and their chances of winning scholarships, achieving university entrance, etc. As well as normal school subjects, there is also a demand for people who can teach the piano and other musical instruments or give extra coaching in various languages.

You can also register with one of the educational agencies:

Truman and Knightley Educational Trust Ltd, or Gabbitas-Thring. (See addresses on pages 225 and 222.)

It is also worth contacting your local education authority — they may have received an inquiry from parents or students. They might also put you on their books as someone who can do supply teaching in an emergency — also paid by the hour.

The average rate for private tuition is from £3.50 to £6 an hour, depending on the level.

Translating/interpreting

The growing emphasis on exports and on our links with the Continent means that this is an expanding field. It is also a highly competitive one, though, and you need to have quite a lot to offer to make a successful living. Most translators work in French and German, for example, so it helps if you are an expert in one of the more unusual languages: there is a great demand at the moment for specialists in Chinese, Japanese and Arabic.

As well as having a language qualification — either a degree or college diploma (eg the Institute of Linguists qualification) — you should also have some other skill or professional qualification to offer. Few firms employ translators for their knowledge of the language alone. They want people who can deal with business correspondence, translate engineering manuals, medical textbooks, technical leaflets, advertising brochures for all kinds of products etc. It always pays to cultivate a special subject and become known as the expert in that field.

To get started initially, try writing to all the translating agencies in the Yellow Pages. Business firms tend to put their work through these agencies, so unless you already have good contacts with a few firms, it is a good idea to get on to the books of an agency. If you fancy literary translating, the best idea again is simply to write round to all the publishing firms — one of them might just happen to have some work going.

Agencies usually pay between £12 and £25 per thousand words, depending on the language. Chinese and Japanese translators are the best paid, and European language translators the worst, with Arabic and Russian specialists

203

somewhere in the middle. If you work for a company direct, without going through an agency, you can charge more. You *can* take on work for private individuals — letters, etc, but it is unlikely to be worthwhile financially, since you can't charge so much.

Being an interpreter requires very special qualities. Apart from having perfect knowledge of two foreign languages, you also need tremendous mental and physical stamina, very quick reactions, above-average intelligence and a good, wide education. These qualities are especially needed for conference work — very few people are good enough, and there are only about 50 conference interpreters in the whole country, but you can also find work at exhibitions, business meetings, as couriers for travel agencies and guides for the London Tourist Board or the British Tourist Authority. (For addresses see pages 220 and 223.)

Writing

Freelance writing is a profession to which many are called but comparatively few are published and from the outset it should be said that unless one is working or has worked on the staff of a newspaper or magazine of some standing, by which a network of professional contacts has been built up, it is a very difficult field for the total newcomer to break into. The best policy then is initially to consider freelance writing as a means of earning extra money over and above that earned from a regular job which will provide the safety-net of a dependable income. If the job is in a related field, such as public relations, advertising or book publishing, so much the better from the point of view of giving the potential writer constant practice at the basics of word craft as well as the opportunity to make new and helpful personal contacts. For the purpose of this section it is assumed that the would-be freelance writer is considering producing articles and short fiction for newspapers or magazines, since first novels, always a favourite with new writers, are notoriously hard to place and, as the current demand for a Public Lending Right shows, even well-established novelists find the financial returns on their work almost impossible to live on.

Unfortunately, many new freelance writers make the

mistake of believing that they have only to write fluently and consistently, with perhaps a welcome seasoning of wit, to be successful in regularly placing their articles. In fact, ease and agility of verbal expression are merely the basic requirements of the journalist's craft and the key to success in placing articles lies firmly in:

1. The choice of a subject to write about.
2. Ensuring that the subject is presented in such a way that it can be readily assimilated into the publication to which you submit it.

Non-fiction subjects

The choice of a subject to write about is a more subtle and demanding undertaking than simply avoiding the submission of cookery articles to political weeklies. Such publications as *The Writers' and Artists' Year Book* list the basic spheres of interest of hundreds of periodicals and newspapers, but after such listings have been scanned for initial guidance, the freelance writer should then study with care several issues of the publication to which he would like to submit material. He should then aim to research and write up a subject which will fall within the sphere of interest of the publication, but which is unlikely to be covered by the full-time or regular part-time contributors to the publication. The reason for this is that although an editor of a newspaper or magazine may think quite highly of a freelance contribution to his publication on, for example, an industrial dispute of national importance, he will not use it if by doing so he will stand on the toes of his regular industrial relations correspondents. Similarly, it is best to avoid initially articles which involve a political or serious economic stance, since these are subjects for which even well-established staff are chosen carefully.

The aim then, is to select a subject which is original and about which one may even have special knowledge in the hope that it will land on an editor's desk as a delightful addition to his page rather than a dubious repetition. For example, while every Arts Page editor will have probably one regular ballet critic/correspondent on his books, his readers will quite likely never hear about that world-championship clog dancing contest at Cleethorpes or that new technological development in the manufacture of block-toed ballet shoes unless these items are submitted by freelance writers who deal with such oblique areas of the dance rather than being employed to make value judgements about specific performances. Sometimes this oblique approach to freelance subject selection can turn into a more permanent proposition if one happens to stumble across a subject which a magazine or newspaper feels it is worth ultimately retaining a correspondent for. A classic example of this is beer, a subject for which at least one national newspaper now retains a correspondent in the manner of the already well-established wine or food correspondent.

Fictional subjects

In the case of writing short fiction a major market is the supply of romantic short stories to women's magazines. Here, although the choice of subject is in principle already determined — either 'love' or romanticised family relationships — the detailed development of the subject needs to be very accurately tailored to a specific magazine. A study of the way romantic fiction is treated in different magazines is even more important nowadays when the new frankness about human relationships has been partly assimilated into some traditional women's magazines and still more positively rejected by others. In certain magazines, aimed at the more mature, housebound married woman, divorce, terminal illness, abortion, explicit pre-marital sex and juvenile delinquency are not acceptable episodes in romantic fiction, while in newer magazines directed at single working women, sexual matters *are* dealt with more explicitly, although the precise degree needs to be judged very expertly.

Many fiction editors on women's magazines receive a steady supply of short stories from literary agents, but it is virtually useless for the new freelance writer to attempt to place work by these means. The vast majority of literary agents will not agree to place short fiction, or indeed any short pieces, for writers who are not already on their books either as novelists or full-length non-fiction writers, but in fact this system is not without its compensations. Fiction editors are quite well aware that many professionally well-established romantic novelists write short stories to a slick and sometimes quite repetitive formula and providing that a new writer observes the strictures on subject matter and length peculiar to the magazine in question, his work may well have the freshness and piquancy which will ensure its acceptance.

Presentation

Having thought out a suitable subject, equal care should be expended on the literary style of the potential piece. Here again, the range of vocabulary, the approach (eg earnest, cynical, folksy) and just as important, the length not only of the piece but of paragraphs, can only be judged by a careful study of the publication to which the piece will be submitted. Major points to observe in the presentation of work may be summarised as follows:

1. Work should be typed, using one and a half or double-spacing on one side of a sheet of paper only. Always retain a carbon copy.
2. Always read your typescript carefully before submitting it and make any corrections, which should be very minor, as clearly as possible.
3. Never submit a manuscript without a covering letter, but keep the letter brief. A covering letter should give the gist of your piece in no more than a sentence or two and draw to the editor's attention any recent or particularly prestigious published work which will help him to get a fuller picture of you.
4. Before writing a covering letter, telephone the publication to obtain the name of the person to whom you should submit the work. This is particularly useful when submitting material to newspapers which tend to be very departmentalised.
5. If your article has any particularly topical connections which give it a limited 'shelf-life' say so in your covering letter and then telephone after several days for a decision. Many articles, rejected by one publication, can quite often be quickly but sensitively revamped and successfuly placed with a rival magazine.
6. When submitting articles to illustrated magazines it is often useful to team up with a freelance photographer, if, and only if, your article directly benefits from illustrations.
7. Never submit uncaptioned photographs and present captions typed on a separate sheet. Remember that two

apposite and technically excellent photographs are better than half a dozen fuzzy snap-shots.

8. If your article is rejected accept the editor's decision cheerfully and courteously and never attempt to get him to change his mind by arguing. Rejecting scores of unsolicited articles by telephone is one of the least pleasant editorial jobs and whether you agree with them or not, editors know what they want. Nor should you expect editors to constructively criticise your work — after all they are running publications, not a school of journalism.

Two final rules for the new freelance writer

1. Never turn a job down, however small and anonymous that job may be and always get commissioned work in on time.

2. Spare no effort when checking that your facts are right. The beginner who acquires a reputation for inaccurate reporting or slip-shod research may as well give up. If a paper or magazine accepts your article, but holds it over for several months, remember to keep abreast of any new developments in the interim: accuracy applies not only to the time of writing, but more important, to the time of publication.

Appendix: Retirement and the Self-Employed Person

F. O. Kemp FCIS, MBIM, former *Director of the Pre-Retirement Association*

The dangers

The desire to be one's own boss and join the self-employed is often very strong after a lifetime spent obeying orders and taking instructions in a large organisation. Ideally, for the person on the verge of retirement, the aims and objectives of running one's own business are to make it relatively trouble-free, to provide a secure additional income and in the case of a man, to allow it to be sold easily after his death for the benefit of his widow. Of course, such businesses cannot be bought at a modest price and anyone with capital to invest who thinks otherwise is a likely target for the professional confidence trickster.

The person retiring from paid employment who is perhaps commuting part of his pension as a lump sum, or is cashing in an endowment policy, must exercise extreme caution in investing the fruits of perhaps a lifetime's work. Any offers of franchise arrangements or purchase of stocks for resale should be viewed with due suspicion, and the advice of the bank manager should be sought in all cases. This sounds basic commonsense, but an article in the *Sunday Times* Business News on confidence tricksters states that 'Phineas Barnum's dictum that there is a fool born every minute was a gross underestimate!' Certainly the experience of the Pre-Retirement Association is that such warnings regarding investment cannot be repeated too often.

For the man or woman who has been an employee throughout life, the risks and stresses of running one's own small business full-time at the age of 60+ can be hazardous.

Take the typical local shopkeeper. He is working 12—16 hours a day. He has to meet ever rising costs — for rates, staff wages, electricity, heating and insurance. He must keep detailed accounts and VAT records. It is unlikely that he will be able to go on holiday with his family, and he dreads being ill. Should he die, his widow would have to cope with the business single-handed, and may decide to try to sell it at a time when prospective buyers will realise she wants to sell out quickly. If she has been living on the business premises she will have to buy a house and face the upheaval of moving at a time when she is still suffering from the shock of bereavement. This is no legacy for any husband to force on to his spouse.

If you are on the verge of retirement you should be looking forward to a period of purposeful activity, and possibly the initial step for someone who still cherishes such ambitions is to take a part-time job in the type of business which interests him. He will then be able to sum up, on the basis of practical experience, the opportunities and problems of buying or starting an enterprise without risking precious capital.

The opportunities

It *is* possible for the employed person to choose a business opportunity to provide an income and interest in retirement provided he plans far enough ahead. There is, for example, a definite need in many places for boarding kennels where people can leave their animals when going on holiday or into hospital. There is also a steady demand for long-term quarantine homes for animals being brought to the UK by owners returning from work overseas. (4500 dogs and 1800 cats a year). But don't underestimate the amount of work or capital involved. In the first place contact the Local Authority. Any kennel or cattery which wishes to keep animals in quarantine must be licensed by the Ministry of Agriculture, Fisheries and Food and the Animal Health Division of the Ministry handling this is at Government Buildings, Hook Rise South, Tolworth, Surbiton, Surrey, KT6 7NF. If you write to this address, the Ministry will supply you with the relevant information and give details of the standards specified for the buildings including the types of material. Also seek out the local veterinary surgeons. They might well know of a business for sale or suggest where one might be started.

One of the advantages with this type of business is not having to invest capital in holding a large stock! Such an enterprise could be started on a small scale by the wife whilst the husband continues his normal occupation until he reaches retirement age. The business could then be expanded when he is available full time to assist his wife.

The retailing business

If you are approaching the age of 60 consider any retail business with a jaundiced eye. As a rough yardstick I would say that today a business with a turnover of £7000—£12000 a year is not economically viable if it has to bear normal overheads. Any retailer with a turnover of more than £10,000 a year must register for Value Added Tax. A supplier will rarely be able to deliver to a small retailer the goods he actually ordered. The haberdasher may request that 75 per cent of men's shirts he orders should be supplied in size 16½. I am told that in practice he is likely to receive only 10 per cent in that size. Often there is only part delivery of orders. Prices change frequently. The retailer must keep up to date with new fashion demands and tastes. He is at the mercy of TV advertisements. The public will expect him to have in stock next day any item they may have seen advertised the previous evening. A newsagent was swamped with orders for a particular book on football which was advertised one evening. Six months later he was still awaiting supplies. The small shopkeeper, despite recent efforts to merge with other small shopkeepers, will always have difficulty in competing with the huge multiple organisations.

Partnerships and consultancy

If you are thinking of entering a partnership discuss any projected arrangement in detail with your solicitor and bank manager. If you have been employed in say the clothing industry and wish to set yourself up as a textile consultant, do not underestimate the cost of keeping yourself up to date.

You will have to buy all the specialist trade journals and not until you leave a large organisation will you fully appreciate the value of having all the secretarial and back-up facilities.

Pensions and National Insurance

In April 1975 a new State Contribution Scheme for the self-employed came into effect (see p103). If you are in doubt concerning your past contribution record in respect of your State Pension the local office of the DHSS will obtain a computer print out of your details from Newcastle. Do not leave this until you are within a few months of the State retirement age. You can also seek advice concerning the desirability of continuing to pay a contribution after normal retiring age in return for enhanced benefits.

Any person within a few years of retirement will not benefit much from the new State Pension Scheme, and the wise man will plan to boost the State Benefits with his own pension arrangements. Specialist companies will offer personal retirement plans which offer adequate pensions with options for lump sum benefits and widow's pensions. It is not widely known that men buying personal pensions, or self-employed annuities can also provide 'reversionary annuities' for their widows. In this case it is an annuity paid to the wife on the husband's death either before or after retirement. The Scottish Widow's Fund is one such company which has promoted a 'reversionary annuity'. Your insurance broker will give unbiassed advice on pension schemes without charging a fee. If you send a stamped addressed envelope to the Pre-Retirement Association (address on p 000) they will send you a list of half a dozen pension advisers from whom you can choose.

The other aspects of retirement

What are the essentials for a successful retirement? Let us give thought to the following, if we are to meet the problems and to explore fully the opportunities which retirement will offer:

1. Good physical and emotional health;
2. Adequate income, substantially beyond subsistence level;
3. Suitable accommodation;

213

4. Congenial associates and neighbours;
5. One or more absorbing interests;
6. An adequate personal philosophy of life.

Finance

The subject which concerns people most, before retirement, is money. Despite galloping inflation, the situation may not be too bad. Sit down (with a large sheet of paper) and write in column one your present budget, then in the next column show the pluses and minuses expected in retirement. Profits, salary, car and expenses from the business will be a minus: pluses will be private pensions plus the state pension, and income from investments. Present outgoings which will be reduced in retirement are obviously travel costs and lower income tax. At home you may have more meals, lighting and heating. Take into account mortgages and insurances which you may have planned to complete at retirement date. At the end of this exercise you will have a fair idea of how your finances will look, and you (and your wife) can decide if you will be able to retire completely or whether you need to look for a part-time job or set up a small business. If you need to supplement your income, remember the earnings limit is now £40 a week each net for you and your wife. If you are a man of 65 or a woman of 60, the State will reduce your State retirement pension if you earn more than this level.

If you are a lucky man whose income is such that you don't need a supplement, then offer your services to an organisation that is looking for voluntary help. Be committed to some job or some person. A garden or a golf course won't get you out of bed, dressed and shaved at 10 am on a frosty January morning, but if you are responsible for driving a car with its boot full of food for the 'Meals on Wheels' service for the aged you'll be there! You will enjoy it and you will get tremendous personal satisfaction from knowing you are being useful to others.

Leisure

Visit your local adult education centre. The centre may conduct a Pre-Retirement Course covering in detail the aspects I have mentioned. Such a course will give you an opportunity to discuss problems with the lecturers and other participants. Reduced rates for pensioners will mean you can take up such things as pottery, painting or old-time dancing for a nominal outlay, and you will meet people of all ages who live near you. Develop the hobby you have been thinking about for years and preferably also take up a completely new one — one that will challenge you and keep that trained mind active. At 60 you can still acquire a degree using the unique service operated by Britain's Open University and by studying at home.

Living arrangements

Where to live in retirement? The cottage by the sea or the country may represent a lifetime's dream but do not be carried away by memories of twenty holidays spent in August at your favourite seaside resort. Go and visit the area in mid-January when half the shops are shut. Do not go to see the town's Director of Tourism. Seek out the Director of Social Services and ask if his area qualifies for the label 'Costa Geriatrica'. Ask him what are the social services and health services for the elderly. You must be practical and accept that eventually you might need such assistance as a home help — especially if by moving away from your home area you will be cutting yourself off from family and friends. Because many South Coast areas have a high population imbalance caused by the retirement migration, the social services, working with limited funds, are unable to meet all the calls made upon them. Similar considerations apply to country areas. With the high cost of petrol an isolated cottage with one bus a day to town could become a virtual prison.

Consider then staying in the area where your family and friends are and which is convenient (but not too convenient!) for grandchildren.

Don't necessarily stay in that large house where you reared the family. Choose a modern bungalow and move into it before you retire. While you are still earning money get all the essentials installed — double glazing and roof insulation. If you can't find or afford a modern bungalow (for you really should plan to avoid stairs in old age) then look around for a suitable property to modernise — remembering that your Local Authority can dispense handsome grants towards modernisation and improvements. Make enquiries with the experts in your area — the local estate agents and the Citizens' Advice Bureau.

The essentials for the retirement home are economic central

VITAL INFORMATION FOR THE SELF-EMPLOYED

and those in a job without a pension

Do you know that the money you save towards a Personal Pension can be **totally** tax exempt? For example, a man aged 49, saving £300 a year, could expect a pension at 65, of £1,659 and with tax relief at the basic rate, his saving costs him **only £198 per annum!**

Do you know you can commute part of your pension for a lump sum that would be **entirely tax free?** And that you can **invest from £100 to £3,000** in a Personal Pension Bond each year (more if you were born before 1916)?

You'll find these, and many more important facts in the new Time Assurance Personal Pension Guide.
A refreshingly simple and easy to understand booklet explaining everything you need to know about Personal Pension Bonds, tax benefits, guarantees, etc. You can have a copy free, together with a personal illustration, simply by writing to:

TIME ASSURANCE SOCIETY, **FREEPOST,** OLDHAM, LANCS. OL8 2YZ.

or telephoning
MANCHESTER: 061-624 7299/9955
LONDON: 01-628 7546
EDINBURGH: 031-556 3895

Time Assurance
The Personal Pension Specialists

heating, privacy, good lighting, sensible electric wiring with plugs half way up the wall, and proper working levels. Make it a safe place to live — more people kill themselves in the home than on the roads! If you find such a home in an area where you are likely to have congenial neighbours and former business associates so much the better.

Health

Everyone should remain as active and lively in retirement as possible. Take as much exercise as your body will permit. This does not mean a sudden conversion to a health and exercise 'kick'. It would be foolish at the age of 60 to start leaping about a squash court after an abstention of 20 years. It would be equally stupid to try to dig in a huge vegetable garden or allotment if you haven't wielded a spade for ages.

There are facilities provided by the local authorities within reach of everyone's pocket. (Isn't it time you benefited from those rates you always complain about?) Local adult education centres provide Yoga and keep-fit classes at very low subsidised prices. For example, London charges about £4 for a three-term year, with reductions for pensioners. Swimming too is an excellent exercise for using muscles and keeping arthritis at bay. If you live in London why not investigate the cost of a subscription to a Health Club, such as the one started in the West End by Debenhams, (the Stores group).

Your wife

A man should remember that his wife's way of life is going to alter as drastically as his when he retires. As one wife said to her husband, 'I did marry you for better or worse — but not for seven lunches a week'. Do not expect your wife to alter her life style — WRVS, Women's Institute, bridge, bingo and the rest — to stay at home to cook you a lunch. Learn to cook for yourself — a useful accomplishment — and let her keep up all her activities. Don't join her clubs and in the interests of matrimonial bliss never serve on the same committee. Join, for instance, your own local bowling club and go your separate ways for part of the day. At least you will have something different to talk to each other about in the evenings.

Now, is all this advice you have had thrust at you worth it, if you look at it in the terms of cost benefit analysis? It is surprising how many people are unaware of life expectancy figures. An average man of 60 can expect to live for another 18 years and the average woman can expect to live and draw the State Pension for 22 years. So an investment in pre-retirement planning should give you a bonus in the years which lie ahead. Such preparation will enable you and your partner to enter this new phase of life with confidence. You will have planned your finances, have a safe suitable house, no bulging waistline, and you will be itching to have time at last to take up all the new activities you have arranged. With the right attitude, retirement can be the most satisfying and fulfilling period of a person's life — the one period in life when the individual has complete freedom of choice to do what he wants to do, at the pace he decides. It is for you to decide in which direction you go.

Good luck!

Note: Mr F O Kemp is the former Director of the Pre-Retirement Association. He was Chairman of the Council of Europe Working Party on Preparation for Retirement. He is co-author of *Looking Ahead — A Guide to Retirement* (Continua Publications) which is available from the Pre-Retirement Association, 19 Undine Street, Tooting, London, SW17 8PP.

Useful Addresses

Before taking the plunge, it is absolutely essential to get all the help and advice you can, especially if you are planning to to invest a lot of money in a business.

Ring one of the specialist bodies listed below, go to the public library, do as much background reading as you have time for, and consult your bank manager (and your solicitor possible). In fact, look before you leap!

Agricultural Central Cooperative Association Ltd *(advice for farmers)*
Agriculture House
Knightsbridge
London SW1
01-235 6296

Agricultural Development Advisory Service *(advice for farmers)*
Ministry of Agriculture, Fisheries and Food
Great Westminster House
Horseferry Road
London SW1
01-216 6311

Agricultural Mortgage Corporation Ltd
Bucklersbury House
3 Queen Victoria Street
London EC4N 8DU
01-248 6711

Association of British Travel Agents
55-57 Newman Street
London W1
01-637 2444

Association of Self-Employed People
279 Church Road
London SE19 2QQ
01-653 4798

Working for Yourself

BBC External Services *(translation/interpreting work)*
Bush House
Strand
London WC2
01-240 3456

Booksellers Association
154 Buckingham Palace Road
London SW1
01-499 6641

British Franchise Association Ltd
15 The Poynings
Iver
Bucks SL0 9DS
0753-653546

The British Hotels, Restaurants and Caterers Association
13 Cork Street
London W1
01-499 6641

British Market Research Bureau Ltd
Saunders House
53 The Mall
London W5
01-567 3060

British Tourist Authority *(interpreting work)*
64 St James's Street
London SW1
01-629 9191

The Building Centre *(building trades work)*
26 Store Street
London WC1
01-637 9001

Building Research Establishment *(building trades work)*
Bucknalls Lane
Watford
WD2 7JR
09273 76612
or
Scottish Laboratory
Kelvin Road
Glasgow
03552 33001
or
Birmingham Engineering and Building Centre
Broad Street
Birmingham
BI 2DB
021-643 1914/8731

The personal touch that could turn your small business into a big success.

Financial help isn't always your sole need when you're planning for the future. Frequently expert advice is just as necessary. And it's all the more welcome when it comes from someone who really has your best interests at heart.

That's why more and more people are bringing their ideas to the Co-operative Bank.

We add the personal touch that can turn ideas into practical realities.

Perhaps we could help *you?*

**Contact, Corporate Business Manager,
The Co-operative Bank, New Century House,
Manchester M60 4EP.
Telephone: 061-834 8687 Ext. 275**

Central Casting Ltd *(for film extras)*
2 Lexington Street
London W1
01-437 5680

Cherry Marshall Model Agency and School
14 Poland Street
London W1
01-437 1610

Cordon Bleu Cookery School
114 Marylebone Lane
London W1
01-935 3503

Council for Small Industries in Rural Areas *(Co SIRA)*
Queen's House
Fish Row
Salisbury SP1 1EX
Salisbury 24411

Department of Industry Small Firms Division
Abell House
John Islip Street
London SW1P 4LN
01-834 4422

Film Artistes Association *(film extras)*
61 Marloes Road
London W8
01-937 4567

Gabbitas — Thring Educational Trust Ltd
6-8 Sackville Street
London W1
01-734 0161/5

Gentle Ghost *(alternative job agency)*
14 Norland Road
London W11
01-603 2871, 602 3719, 603 2865

Hairdressing Council
17 Spring Street
London W2
01-402 6367

Highlands and Islands Development Board
6 Castle Wynd
Inverness
Scotland IV2 3ED

Working for Yourself

Hotel and Catering Industry Training Board
PO Box 18
Central Square
Wembley
Middlesex
01-902 8865

Industrial and Commercial Finance Corporation (ICFC)
91 Waterloo Road
London SE1 8XP

Institute of Linguists
29a Highbury Grove
London N5 2EA

Institute of Small Business
1 Whitehall Place
London SW1A 2HD

International Air Transport Association *(licensing for travel agents)*
West London Air Terminal
Cromwell Road
London SW7 4ED
01-370 4255

Lapidary Publications
84 High Street
Broadstairs
Kent
0843 64083

Licensed Trade Development Association
42 Portman Square
London N1H 0BB

London Tourist Board
26 Grosvenor Gardens
London SW1
01-730 0791

Lucy Clayton Fashion School and Model Agency
168 Brompton Road
London SW3
01-581 0024

Market Research Society
15 Belgrave Square
London SW1X 8PF
01-235 4709

National Farmers' Union
Agriculture House
Knightsbridge
London SW1
01-235 5077

National Federation of Retail Newsagents
2 Bridewell Place
London EC4
01-353 6816

National Federation of Self Employed
St Anne's Road West
Lytham St Annes
Lancashire

National Research Development Corporation
66 Victoria Street
London SW1

**The National Union of Small Shopkeepers of Great Britain
and Northern Ireland**
Westminster Buildings
Theatre Square
Nottingham NGL 6LH
Nottingham 45046

Northern Ireland Development Agency
Maryfield
100 Belfast Road
Hollywood
County Down
Hollywood 4232

Part-Time Careers Ltd *(mainly secretarial, research, editorial work)*
10 Golden Square
London W1
01-437 3103

Pre-School Playgroups Association
Alford House
Aveline Street
London SE11
01-582 8871
or
Room 417
93 Hope Street
Glasgow G2

Research Bureau Ltd *(market research)*
PO Box 203
Green Bank
Wapping
London E1 9PA
01-488 1366

Scottish Development Agency
Small Business Division
102 Telford Road
Edinburgh
031-343 1911

Society of Indexers
28 Johns Avenue
London NW4 4EN
01-203 0929

London Street Markets

Camden Passage Market
Upper Street
Islington, London N1
Craft stalls Tuesday to Saturday, costing £3 per day
Ring Derrick Moss 01-226 0971 and
01-359 2328

Dingwalls Market
Camden Lock
Camden High Street
London NW1
Saturdays and Sundays only, £3 per day Christmas to Easter, £4 the
rest of the year
Ring 01-485 7963

Portobello Road Market
Notting Hill Gate
London W11
£2.60 per day, £5.75 per week Apply to Kensington Town Hall,
Market Dept, Kensington High Street,
London W8. 01-937 5464

Translators' Association
Society of Authors
84 Drayton Gardens
London SW10
01-373 6642

Truman and Knightley Educational Trust Ltd *(educational agency)*
76 & 78 Notting Hill Gate
London W11
01-727 1242

Ugly Agency *(model agency)*
6 Windmill Street
London W1
01-636 9672

Universal Aunts Ltd *(odd jobs of all kinds)*
36 Walpole Street
London SW3
01-730 9834

Welsh Development Agency
Treforest Industrial Estate
Pontypridd
Mid-Glamorgan
Treforest 2666

We People *(alternative job agency)*
92 Tavistock Road
London W11
01-727 1228

Small Firms Information Centres

The Centres, set up by the Department of Industry, provide a free information service for small firms, and are able to provide information on any type of business problem. They also produce a number of useful pamphlets.

London and South Eastern Region
65 Buckingham Palace Road
London SW1W 0QX
01-828 2384

South Western Region
Colston Centre
Colston Avenue
Bristol BS1 4UB
Bristol 294546

Northern Region
22 Newgate Shopping Centre
Newcastle upon Tyne NE1 5RH
Newcastle 25353

North Western Region
Peter House
Oxford Street
Manchester M1 5AN
061-832 5282
and

226

Working for Yourself

1 Old Hall Street
Liverpool L3 9HJ
051-236 5756

Yorkshire and Humberside Region
Royal Exchange House
Boar Lane
Leeds LS1 5NF

East Midlands Region
48-50 Maid Marian Way
Nottingham NG1 6GF
Nottingham 49791

West Midland Region
53 Stephenson Street
Birmingham B2 4DH
021-643 3344

Eastern Region
35 Wellington Street
Luton LU1 2SB
Luton 29215

Scotland
57 Bothwell Street
Glasgow G2 6TU
041-248 6014

Wales
16 St David's House
Wood Street
Cardiff CF1 1ER
Cardiff 396116

Bibliography

Part 1

Business of Your Own Today, by B Fraser Harrison (World's Work)
Buying and Running Your Own Business, by Ian Ford (Business Books)
Company Law, 5th edition, by M C Oliver (Macdonald & Evans)
Croner's Reference Book for the Self-Employed, ed by Daphne McAra (Croner Publication Ltd)
Daily Telegraph Guide to Income Tax, by B Budibent (Collins)
Direct Mail and Direct Response Promotion, by Christian Brann (Kogan Page)
Everyday Credit Checking, S Barzman (Thomas Y Crowell, New York)
Financing of Small Business, by J Bates (Sweet & Maxwell)
Going Solo, by William Perry and Derek Jones (BBC Publications)
A Guide to Franchising, by Martin Mendelsohn (Pergamon Press)
The Hambro Tax Guide, by A S Silke and W I Sinclair (Macdonald and Jane, published annually)
How to Read a Balance Sheet, 5th revised edition (ILO)
How To Start Your Own Craft Business, by H Genfan and L Taetzsch (Watson Guptill, New York)
Management of Trade Credit, by T G Hutson and J Butterworth (Gower Press)
Managing for Results, by Peter F Drucker (Pan Books)
More Profit from Your Stock, by E A Jensen, 2nd edition (available from the author, 39 Withdean Crescent, Brighton)
Occupation: Self-Employed, by Rosemary Pettit (Wildwood House)
Run Your Own Business, by Peter Douglas (Dent)
Small Firms Information Centres Publications 1—20, by various authors (Small Firms Information Centres)
Success in Bookkeeping for the Small Business, by G Whitehead (John Murray)
Success In Principles of Accounting, by G Whitehead (John Murray)
VAT Explained, by John Chown (Kogan Page)

Part 2

British Qualifications, ed by Barbara Priestley (Kogan Page)
Buying a Shop, by E A Jensen

228

A Catering Business of Your Own, by E M Turner, rev ed R H Johnson (Barrie & Jenkins)

Chaffer's Handbook to Hall Marks on Gold and Silver Plate (William Reeves)

Choice of Careers Booklets (HMSO)

The Fruit Garden Displayed (Royal Horticultural Society)

Gems Magazine (Lapidary Publications)

A Guide to the Building Regulations, by A J Elder (Architectural Press)

The Guide to Franchising, by Martin Mendelsohn (Pergamon Press)

How To Become a Photographic Model, by Jean Campbell Dallas (Pelham Books)

How To Form a Playgroup (BBC Publications)

How to Write a Story and Sell It, by St Johns (Kennikat Press)

Jewellery Making and Design, by Augustus F Rose and Antonio Cirino (Dover Publications)

Money and Your Retirement, by E V Eves (Pre-Retirement Association)

Mother's Help, for Busy Mothers and Playgroup Leaders, (ed) Susan Dickinson (Collins)

Pottery, by Emmanuel Cooper (MacDonald Educational)

The Other Careers — Earning a Living in the Arts and Media, by Mike Bygrave, Joan Goodman and John Fordham (Wildwood House)

Restoring Old Junk, by Michele Brown (Lutterworth Press)

The Retirement Book, ed by M Pilch (Hamish Hamilton)

Running Your Own Hotel, by Arthur Neil (Barrie and Jenkins)

Simple Pottery, by Kenneth Drake (Studio Vista)

Soft Furnishing — A Practical Manual for the Home Upholsterer, by A V White (Routledge & Kegan Paul)

Technical Translator's Manual, (ed) J B Sykes (Aslib)

The Vegetable Garden Displayed (Royal Horticultural Society)

'Vogue' Guide to Knitting, Crochet and Macrame (Collins)

'Vogue' Sewing Book (Butterick Pub Co)

Working with Gemstones, by V A Firsoff (David & Charles)

Working with Languages (Institute of Linguists)

Writers' and Artists' Yearbook (A & C Black)

Writing for the BBC (BBC Publications)

Writing for Television in the Seventies, by M Hulke (A & C Black)

You Too Can Write for Money, by Harvey Day (A Thomas)

Advertisers Index